POETRY
AND PROSE
APPRECIATION
FOR OVERSEAS
STUDENTS

By the same author

Sixty Steps to Précis:
A New Approach to Summary Writing
for Overseas Students

POETRY AND PROSE APPRECIATION FOR OVERSEAS STUDENTS

L. G. Alexander

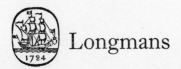 Longmans

LONGMANS, GREEN & CO LTD
48 Grosvenor Street, London W.1

*Associated companies, branches and
representatives throughout
the world*

© L. G. Alexander 1963
First published 1963

Printed in Great Britain by
Western Printing Services Ltd, Bristol

CONTENTS

ACKNOWLEDGMENTS

We are grateful to the following for permission to include copyright material:

George Allen & Unwin Ltd. and Liveright Publishing Corporation, New York, for an extract from *The Conquest of Happiness* by Bertrand Russell; Edward Arnold Ltd. and Harcourt, Brace & World, Inc. for an extract from *Abinger Harvest* by E. M. Forster; the author for an extract from *Day's End* by H. E. Bates; Jonathan Cape Ltd. for extracts from *The Old Man and the Sea* by Ernest Hemingway, *Portrait of the Artist as a Young Man* by James Joyce, *Darkness at Noon* by Arthur Koestler, and *Meaning and Purpose* by Kenneth Walker; Chatto & Windus Ltd. for an extract from *Possible Words* by J. B. S. Haldane; Cambridge University Press for an extract from *Man on his Past* by Herbert Butterfield; J. M. Dent & Sons Ltd. for the poem *To a Poet a Thousand Years Hence* by James Elroy Flecker and an extract from *Portrait of the Artist as a Young Dog* by Dylan Thomas; Mrs. Hilda L. Edwards for an extract from *Thinking to Some Purpose* by Susan Stebbing; Faber & Faber Ltd. and Coward McCann Inc. for an extract from *Lord of the Flies* by William Golding; Faber & Faber Ltd. and Harcourt, Brace & World Inc. for an extract from *Modern Education and the Classics* by T. S. Eliot; Faber & Faber Ltd. and Random House Inc. for 'Look Stranger' and 'Oh, What is that Sound' from *Collected Shorter Poems* by W. H. Auden; the author and Holt, Rinehart & Winston Inc. for 'Tree at my Window' from *The Complete Poems of Robert Frost*; Hamish Hamilton Ltd. and *The New Yorker* for an extract from 'My Life and Hard Times' by James Thurber from *The Thurber Carnival*;

The Trustees of the Hardy Estate, Macmillan & Co. Ltd. and The Macmillan Company, New York, for the poem *He Never Expected Much—A Consideration on My 86th Birthday* by Thomas Hardy; Mr. Tom Harrisson, D.S.O., O.B.E., F.R.G.S., Curator of the Sarawak Museum, for an extract from his broadcast talk *Ghosts and Dreams*, which appeared in the *Listener* on 29th December 1956; Rupert Hart-Davis Ltd. for the poem *The Dead Crab* by Andrew Young; William Heinemann Ltd. and Little, Brown & Co. for an extract from *A Buyer's Market* by Anthony Powell; the author for an extract from *Coming to London* by Christopher Isherwood, which appeared in the *London Magazine*, Vol. 3, No. 8, August 1956; the Estate of the late Mrs. Frieda Lawrence, Laurence Pollinger Ltd. and The Viking Press Inc. for an extract from *England, My England* by D. H. Lawrence; the author for an extract from *Sagittarius Rising* by Cecil Lewis; the Literary Trustees of Walter de la Mare and the Society of Authors as their representative for *The Listeners* and *The Spark*; the author, William Heinemann Ltd. and Doubleday & Co. Inc. for extracts from 'The Razor's Edge' and 'The Luncheon' from *The Complete Short Stories*, Vol. I, by W. Somerset Maugham; Methuen & Co. Ltd. for an extract from *Why We Hate Insects* by Robert Lynd; John Murray Ltd. and Beacon Press, Boston, for an extract from *Perseus and the Wind* by Freya Stark; the author for an extract from *The Genius* by Frank O'Connor; the author's executors for an extract from *Animal Farm* by George Orwell; Oxford University Press for the poem *Heaven Haven* by Gerard Manley Hopkins; Oxford University Press and Oxford University Press, Inc. for an extract from *Civilization on Trial* by Arnold Toynbee; Penguin Books Ltd. for extracts from *The English Penal System* by W. Elkin, *An Introduction to Jung's Psychology* by Frieda Fordham, *Memory* by I. M. L. Hunter, *European Painting and Sculpture* by E. Newton and *An Introduction to Modern Architecture* by J. H. Richards; the author for an extract from *The Future of the Writer* by J. B. Priestley; the author and the Hogarth Press Ltd. for an extract from 'Question and Answer' from *A Contest of Ladies* by William Sansom; Sidgwick & Jackson Ltd. and Dodd, Mead & Co. for the poem 'The Dead' from *The Collected Poems of Rupert Brooke*, reprinted by permission, copyright 1915 by Dodd, Mead & Company, copyright 1943 by Edward Marsh; The Society of Authors as the literary representative of the Estate of the late Miss Katherine Mansfield for an extract from *The Garden Party*; the Society of Authors, Dr. John Masefield o.m. and The Macmillan Company, New York, for the poems *Cargoes* and *Sea Fever*; the author's executors for an extract from 'The Country of the Blind' from *The Time Machine and Other Stories* by H. G. Wells; Mr. Leonard Woolf for an extract from *The Waves* by Virginia Woolf; and Mrs. Yeats and Macmillan & Co. Ltd. for 'The Wild Swans at Coole' and 'An Irish Airman Forsees His Death' from *The Collected Poems of W. B. Yeats*.

A NOTE TO THE TEACHER

Literary Appreciation and the Student

No subject can be more bewildering to the advanced learner of English than 'Literary Appreciation'. Even when the student is writing in his mother-tongue and reading literature by authors whose work may be familiar to him, appreciation is often a difficult task. When the student is faced with literature in a foreign language the problem becomes all the more acute. He is in command of a relatively limited vocabulary and yet is required to comment intelligently on works which may tax his powers of comprehension to the utmost. Furthermore, a certain vagueness surrounds the whole subject: the student frequently does not know what to say about a piece of writing he has read. He may succeed in enjoying and understanding a poem or a prose-passage, but the necessity to explain *why* he has enjoyed it is usually far beyond his powers.

This book may be found to supply the answer to precisely this sort of problem since it sets out to provide the student with a clear, well-defined method for appreciating poetry and prose. If the student is trained along the lines suggested in this book he should be better equipped to get the most out of what he reads and should have little difficulty in writing in an interesting way about pieces he has enjoyed.

How to use this book

Poetry and Prose Appreciation should be used over a period of two years with adult students or with senior pupils in secondary schools preparing for the English literature paper of the Cambridge Proficiency in English examination or for G.C.E. 'O' level. Examinations apart, the book may be found useful as an introduction to the appreciation of literature with any class of more advanced students who need to be given the opportunity to read original texts. When this is the case, however, the book should never be used as a short-cut to literature or as a substitute, but as an *aid to reading*, a stepping-stone to more complete works.

The inclusion of the word *Appreciation* as distinct from *Criticism* in the title of this book has been deliberate. Teachers sometimes give their students the impression that they are in a position to 'criticize' fine creative writing in the belief that this makes appreciation 'exciting'. For a beginner, no approach could be more misleading, for in this way the student is led to assume that in order to be original he must find 'something wrong' with everything he reads. It is hardly necessary to point out that a student must learn to *appreciate* long before he can *criticize*. Only then will we be saved the embarrassment of being informed by our students that, say, a sonnet by Shakespeare is 'quite a nice poem'.

The Enjoyment of Literature

The key to true appreciation is, of course, enjoyment and this depends largely on the teacher's own attitude to literature in general. It is just as easy to be carried away by your own enthusiasm and to race through dozens of pieces (leaving the class far behind you) as it is to work too slowly and too seriously, treating every passage as a potential examination text. This book is not meant to be a handy anthology for the over-enthusiastic teacher, but neither is it intended to be a dry-as-dust textbook. It may not prove necessary for the teacher to plod solidly through every exercise provided and he may easily adapt the book to suit the needs of his class, always bearing in mind that enjoyment is the first step to understanding and appreciating. A class will often readily respond to material which, at first glance, seems unpromising. A good example of this occurs in Browning's 'Soliloquy in a Spanish Cloister'. The poem looks long and formidable and is written in a difficult style. But it is surprising how much enjoyment a lively reading of it will afford a class even if they have only a general idea of what it is about. Good reading is important and should not be considered as an irksome duty. Apart from reading aloud occasionally, the teacher may supply the class with a little background information about the author and his work where possible. This gives added interest to the lesson and helps the class to become receptive so that appreciation becomes a pleasure.

The Stages of Learning

Much the same pattern is followed in both parts of the book. In the first instance, the student is taught how to read and understand. In the case of poetry this is often very difficult and the teacher should do all he can to discourage his pupils from reading carelessly and arriving at hasty, ill-informed conclusions. Once the student has learnt to make sense out of what he is reading, he is, as it were, taken into the author's workshop and is taught how to recognize some of the main techniques that writers employ. Only when he has fully grasped how a writer works is he in a position to write appreciation on his own. A simple key summing up all that has been learned precedes each selection of pieces.

Vocabulary Lists

The vocabulary lists appended to each poem or prose-passage are intended to help the student who is working on his own. In some instances these lists may be found to be inadequate since at this stage there is no real way of gauging difficulty. By and large, however, explanations have been given for archaic expressions, especially difficult words, phrases or idioms, and in places where the syntax is distorted. A great many of these words and phrases need not be added to the student's active vocabulary. The differentiation between essential and inessential words has been left entirely to the teacher's discretion.

PART I   POETRY

No attempt has been made to confine the selection to any particular period or to poems which the student will never have seen before. It is no accident that some of the best-known poems in the English language have been included. While learning to appreciate poetry, the student will also have before him a sample of the work of some of the greatest poets who have written in the English language.

Teachers may find it useful to conduct the simple test suggested on page 3 as a way of introducing students to poetry appreciation. The test consists in allowing students to express in writing and anonymously their own interpretation of a poem and then having their views read back to them by the teacher. This test is of value as it enables students to understand immediately that it is very easy to misread a poem completely. At the same time the student may perceive that a poem sometimes communicates at various levels and no single meaning can be attached to it. The poem by Blake which has been chosen is highly suitable for this purpose. It is short, relatively easy to read and has both a simple and a complex meaning. Occasionally the teacher may devote a lesson to conducting similar tests with other poems in the book as students often find it enjoyable to work in this way.

PART II   PROSE

Although, naturally enough for a student, prose is easier to understand than poetry, it is far more difficult to appreciate because the means a writer uses are less obvious. Furthermore, no prose-extract can ever be as complete and self-contained as a poem. For this reason it has been found necessary to alter the general arrangement of Part II slightly without, however, changing the basic pattern which is followed in the poetry section. Chapter I of Part II is devoted to distinguishing types of prose because it is absolutely essential for students to understand how Narrative and Description differ from Argument. Only when they have done so will they be able to appreciate what they are reading. Whereas in the poetry section all four chapters follow on logically from each other so that it is necessary to work through the first three chapters before coming on to appreciation, in the prose section each chapter is treated as a complete unit. Thus it is possible for the teacher to begin with any chapter he wishes after he has completed the first one. It is inadvisable, however, to begin with the last chapter ('Argument') as this is likely to be found difficult. Also, the method for appreciation differs in many important respects from that learned in all the other sections of the book.

Part I

POETRY

I

WHAT IS IT ABOUT?

READING A POEM

You may have found from your reading of poetry in your own language that you can often enjoy a poem without fully understanding its meaning. It is possible to pay more attention to the *way* a poet says something rather than to *what* he actually has to say. Enjoyment, however, must not be confused with appreciation. It is one thing to gain pleasure from a poem and quite another to be able to say why you liked it. Before you can say why you like a poem, it is first necessary to understand its meaning well. This is not always easy, as a simple experiment in class will show.

Read the poem below as carefully as you can and then write briefly on a piece of paper what you think it means. When you have finished, hand the paper to your teacher. The teacher will then read aloud the answers that have been given by every member of the class. Later, you may discuss the meaning of the poem.

> O rose, thou art sick!
> The invisible worm
> That flies in the night,
> In the howling storm,
>
> Has found out thy bed
> Of crimson joy,
> And his dark secret love
> Does thy life destroy.

Vocabulary

    howling: crying out as if in pain.
    crimson: deep red.

The answers you heard may have helped you to understand how a single poem may have different meanings for different people. Some of the answers given may have been quite wrong. But you must have noticed that none of the 'right' answers were exactly the same.

This does not mean, of course, that all poems can be interpreted in a wide variety of ways. Quite often a poem may have a meaning which is simple and obvious: it may just tell a story or describe a scene. A piece of writing need not always have a 'deep' meaning simply because it happens to be a poem.

To understand a poem you must read it carefully and should observe three important rules:

1. Do not read lazily so that you misread the poem altogether.

2. Always look for a simple explanation and do not be afraid to express it.

3. As far as you can, avoid putting your own ideas and feelings into the poem. Examine closely what the poet has actually written.

Let us see how these rules apply to the following poem:

[1] *Break, Break, Break*

Break, break, break,
   On thy cold grey stones, O Sea!
And I would that my tongue could utter
   The thoughts that arise in me.

O well for the fisherman's boy,   5
   That he shouts with his sister at play!
O well for the sailor lad,
   That he sings in his boat on the bay!

And the stately ships go on
   To their haven under the hill;   10
But O for the touch of a vanish'd hand,
   And the sound of a voice that is still!

Break, break, break,
   At the foot of thy crags, O Sea!
But the tender grace of a day that is dead   15
   Will never come back to me.

ALFRED, LORD TENNYSON

Vocabulary

  I would (l. 3): I wish.
  O well (l. 5): i.e., it is well.
  stately (l. 9): dignified.
  haven (l. 10): harbour.
  crags (l. 14): steep rocks.

1. If this poem were read carelessly it might be taken to be simply about the sea.

2. But the lines

    And I would that my tongue could utter
      The thoughts that arise in me.

  show us that the poet is sad. The lines

    But O for the touch of a vanish'd hand,
      And the sound of a voice that is still!

  tell us why he is sad. In other words, the poet is unhappy because he has lost someone he loves, whereas the sea, the people near it (the fisherman's boy and the sailor lad) and the 'stately ships' are unaware and untroubled, so the poet can draw no comfort from them. This is the simple explanation of the poem.

3. If we try to put our own ideas into the poem, we might be led to assume that the poet is sad because someone he loves has been drowned. As this idea is not expressed or implied it cannot be true.

FINDING THE MEANING

After a careful reading of a poem we should be in a position to give its general meaning, its detailed meaning, and to say something about the intentions of the writer.

General Meaning. This should be expressed simply in one, or at the most two sentences. It should be based on a reading of the *whole* poem. Very often, but not always, a poem's title will give you some indication of its general meaning.

Detailed Meaning. This should be given stanza by stanza, but you should *not* paraphrase the poem or worry about the meaning of individual words. The detailed meaning may be written as a continuous paragraph, but you must take every care to be accurate and to express yourself in simple sentences. Similarly you must pay special attention to your prose style. Do not express yourself clumsily or write a list each sentence of which begins with 'In the first stanza . . .', 'In the second stanza . . .' etc. You should show how the poet begins, how he develops his theme and then how he concludes it. If a poem is not divided into stanzas, you should make some rough attempt in your reading to divide the lines into fairly self-contained groups.

Intention. Every poem conveys an experience and attempts to arouse certain feelings in the reader. When you have read a poem and given its general and detailed meaning, you should try to decide what feelings the poet is trying to arouse in you. A poem may affect different people in a great variety of ways and it is often impossible to define a poet's 'true' intentions. Your interpretation of a poet's aims is, therefore, largely a personal matter, but at the same time it should never be far-fetched. It is, however, most important to explain what you have understood a poet's purpose to be. Just as it is impossible to give the meaning of a poem if you have not read it carefully, it is impossible to appreciate the poem if you are unable to define the poet's intentions.

Read carefully the poem below and then write its general and detailed meaning. After that try to decide what the poet's intentions are. What feelings is he trying to arouse in you? What is he setting out to do? When you have given your own view of the poem, read the paragraphs that follow and see how near you came to understanding it.

[2] *Cargoes*

Quinquireme of Nineveh from distant Ophir
Rowing home to haven in sunny Palestine,
With a cargo of ivory,
And apes and peacocks,
Sandalwood, cedarwood, and sweet white wine. 5

Stately Spanish galleon coming from the Isthmus,
Dipping through the Tropics by the palm-green shores,
With a cargo of diamonds,
Emeralds, amethysts,
Topazes, and cinnamon, and gold moidores. 10

Dirty British coaster with a salt-caked smoke-stack
Butting through the Channel in the mad March days,
With a cargo of Tyne coal,
Road-rail, pig-lead,
Firewood, iron-ware, and cheap tin trays.

JOHN MASEFIELD

Vocabulary

quinquireme (l. 1): ancient ship with five rows of oars.
galleon (l. 6): an old type of warship or trading ship.
emeralds, amethysts, topazes (ll. 9-10): precious stones.
cinammon (l. 10): a sweet-smelling spice.
moidores (l. 10): gold coins.
smoke-stack (l. 11): funnel.
butting (l. 12): pushing with the head in the way a goat does.
pig-lead (l. 14): blocks of lead.

General meaning, detailed meaning and intention. In this poem, Masefield describes the various cargoes that have been carried by ships in three different ages.

The poet begins by describing two of the biggest and most beautiful ships of the past. The earlier of the two ships is a quinquireme; the later a 'stately Spanish galleon'. Both are pictured in bright sunshine carrying goods which, though different in kind, were rare and precious. The quinquireme comes laden with ivory, strange animals and fine wood; the galleon with precious stones. The ship described in the last stanza is quite different. It belongs to modern times and is small ('a coaster') and dirty. It is on a short journey across the English Channel in bad weather with its cheap and useful cargo of coal, metal, and firewood.

The poet does not simply set out to describe cargoes but to make us consider how the present differs from the past. In the past, the goods that were highly prized were beautiful, rare, and comparatively useless; in the present, the goods are ugly, common and useful. From the way the poet describes these three different ships, we can see that he implies that modern times are less beautiful than former times.

EXERCISES ON FINDING THE MEANING

Answer the questions on each of the poems that follow. When doing so, bear in mind the example you have just read.

[3] *Ozymandias*

I met a traveller from an antique land
Who said: Two vast and trunkless legs of stone
Stand in the desert . . . Near them, on the sand,
Half-sunk, a shattered visage lies, whose frown,
And wrinkled lip, and sneer of cold command,   5
Tell that its sculptor well those passions read
Which yet survive, stamped on these lifeless things,
The hand that mocked them, and the heart that fed:
And on the pedestal these words appear:
'My name is Ozymandias, king of kings: 10
Look on my works, ye Mighty, and despair!'
Nothing beside remains. Round the decay
Of that colossal wreck, boundless and bare
The lone and level sands stretch far away. .

PERCY BYSSHE SHELLEY

Vocabulary

trunkless legs (l. 2): the legs are still standing, but the upper part of the body (the trunk) has been cut off.

shattered visage (l. 4): face, broken to pieces.
pedestal (l. 9): base of statue.
ye (l. 11): you.
colossal (l. 13): very big.
boundless (l. 13): unending.

QUESTIONS

1. Where was the statue seen and who saw it?
2. What words tell us that the statue was broken to pieces?
3. '. . . its sculptor well those passions read.' What passions?
4. Briefly describe the character of Ozymandias.
5. Write the general and detailed meaning of the poem and what you consider to be the poet's intention.

[4] *The Ancient Mariner*

The lines that follow are taken from a long poem in which one of the sailors shoots an albatross and thus brings a curse on the ship. These lines occur shortly after the sailor kills the bird as the ship enters the Pacific Ocean.

> The fair breeze blew, the white foam flew,
> The furrow followed free;
> We were the first that ever burst
> Into that silent sea.
>
> Down dropt the breeze, the sails dropt down,   5
> 'Twas sad as sad could be;
> And we did speak only to break
> The silence of the sea!
>
> All in a hot and copper sky,
> The bloody Sun, at noon,   10
> Right up above the mast did stand,
> No bigger than the Moon.
>
> Day after day, day after day,
> We stuck, nor breath nor motion;
> As idle as a painted ship   15
> Upon a painted ocean.

Water, water, everywhere,
And all the boards did shrink;
Water, water, everywhere
Nor any drop to drink.

S. T. COLERIDGE

Vocabulary

furrow (l. 2): deep line made in the earth by a plough. Here, of
course, the word refers to the water behind the moving ship.
'Twas (l. 6): i.e., it was.

QUESTIONS

1. Quote the lines that tell us that no other ship had ever sailed
   in this sea.

   Which line tells us that the wind suddenly stopped blowing?

3. Explain these lines as fully as you can:

   As idle as a painted ship
   Upon a painted ocean.

4. Write the general and detailed meaning of the poem and what
   you consider to be the poet's intention.

[5] *Lucy*

She dwelt among the untrodden ways
    Beside the springs of Dove,
A Maid whom there were none to praise
    And very few to love:

A violet by a mossy stone   5
    Half hidden from the eye!
—Fair as a star, when only one
    Is shining in the sky.

She lived unknown, and few could know
    When Lucy ceased to be;   10
But she is in her grave, and, oh,
    The difference to me!

WILLIAM WORDSWORTH

Vocabulary
   dwelt (l. 1): lived.
   untrodden (l. 1): unfrequented, little known.

QUESTIONS

1. What does the poet tell us about Lucy's character?
2. Why does he compare her to a violet and then to a star?
3. Write the general and detailed meaning of the poem and what you consider to be the poet's intention.

[6] *To a Poet a Thousand Years Hence*

I who am dead a thousand years,
   And wrote this sweet archaic song,
Send you my words for messengers
   The way I shall not pass along.

I care not if you bridge the seas,   5
   Or ride secure the cruel sky,
Or build consummate palaces
   Of metal or of masonry.

But have you wine and music still,
   And statues and a bright-eyed love,   10
And foolish thoughts of good and ill,
   And prayers to them who sit above?

How shall we conquer? Like a wind
   That falls at eve our fancies blow,
And old Mæonides the blind   15
   Said it three thousand years ago.

O friend unseen, unborn, unknown,
   Student of our sweet English tongue,
Read out my words at night, alone:
   I was a poet, I was young.   20

Since I can never see your face,
   And never shake you by the hand,

I send my soul through time and space
To greet you. You will understand.

JAMES ELROY FLECKER

Vocabulary

archaic (l. 2): ancient.
consummate (l. 7): perfect.
masonry (l. 8): stonework.
eve (l. 14): evening.

QUESTIONS

1. Why does the poet call his poem an 'archaic song'?
2. How do we know that the poet is not interested in material progress? What does interest him?
3. What is the meaning of

Like a wind
That falls at eve our fancies blow . . . ?
Why does the poet quote this line?

4. The poem concludes with the line 'You will understand'. What will he understand?
5. Give the general and detailed meaning of the poem and what you consider to be the poet's intention.

[7] *On His Eighty-sixth Birthday*

Well, World, you have kept faith with me,
    Kept faith with me;
Upon the whole you have proved to be
    Much as you said you were.
Since as a child I used to lie   5
Upon the leaze and watch the sky,
Never, I own, expected I
    That life would all be fair.

'Twas then you said, and since have said,
    Times since have said,   10
In that mysterious voice you shed
    From clouds and hills around:

'Many have loved me desperately,
Many with smooth serenity,
While some have shown contempt of me   15
    Till they dropped underground.

'I do not promise overmuch,
    Child; overmuch;
Just neutral-tinted haps and such,'
    You said to minds like mine.   20
Wise warning for your credit's sake!
Which I for one failed not to take,
And hence could stem such strain and ache
    As each year might assign.

                         THOMAS HARDY

Vocabulary

    leaze (l. 6): pasture, meadow.
    I own (l. 7): I confess.
    serenity (l. 14): calm.
    haps (l. 19): happenings.
    stem (l. 23): make headway against (tide, current, etc.).

QUESTIONS

1. Why is the poet not displeased with the world?
2. What was the world's 'wise warning'?
3. How did this warning help the poet?
4. Give the general and detailed meaning of the poem and what you consider to be the poet's intention.

2

HOW IT IS DONE

So far we have confined ourselves to a study of *what* a poem says. This is the first step to understanding *how* a poet expresses himself. 'Literary Appreciation' is no more than this. Finding the meaning of a poem and the intentions of the writer are simply the means.

It is hard to define exactly what a poem is and to state why it gives us pleasure. The subject-matter of a poem is not necessarily the most important thing about it. Any poem sets out to convey a great deal more than an idea and it is this that distinguishes it from prose. The delight we get when reading poetry often comes from its musical qualities, or from the striking way a poet uses words. But this can only be a partial explanation, for poetry does not follow hard and fast rules: every poem is unique and has special qualities of its own. Some of these, however, are properties common to all poetry. If we are to appreciate poetry, it is necessary to learn how to recognize these 'special qualities'. They are called *devices* and can be found when we analyse a poem. For the sake of convenience, devices may be divided into three groups: structural, sense, and sound. When writing an appreciation of poetry, it is not enough to be able to point out devices. You must always explain what effect they have and how they help the poet to fulfil his intentions.

In the analysis of devices that follows, all the examples have been drawn from the poems you studied in the preceding chapter.

STRUCTURAL DEVICES

Contrast, illustration, repetition: these indicate the way a whole poem has been built and become apparent as soon as the meaning of the poem has been found.

Contrast. This is one of the most common of all structural devices. It occurs when we find two completely opposite pictures side by side. Sometimes the contrast is immediately obvious and sometimes implied.

Contrast of the most direct kind can be found in the poem *Cargoes*, where a direct comparison is made between ancient and modern times: the last ship differs greatly from the first two.

In the lines from *The Ancient Mariner* there is contrast between the motion of the ship which was travelling so quickly that it 'burst into that silent sea' and the complete lack of motion which immediately follows: 'Down dropt the breeze, the sails dropt down'.

Similarly in *Ozymandias* the great broken statue is seen against the background of the vast and empty desert:

> Round the decay
> Of that colossal wreck, boundless and bare
> The lone and level sands stretch far away.

In the two poems *Break, Break, Break* and *Lucy* the contrast between life and death is implied. Turn back to both poems and see if you can find out how this contrast has been drawn.

Illustration. This is an example which usually takes the form of a vivid picture by which a poet may make an idea clear. Pictures of this sort occur in all the poems you have studied.

Cargoes consists of three such pictures each of which represents the poet's view of different ages. The poet means to show that bygone times were refined and gracious and that modern times are squalid: the quinquireme is 'rowing home to haven', the galleon 'dipping through the tropics' while the 'dirty British coaster' is 'butting through the channel'.

In *Break, Break, Break* there are pictures of the fisherman's boy, the sailor lad and the stately ships. It is by these means that the poet stresses the fact that life goes on when someone dies or suffers.

The picture given in *Ozymandias* illustrates the idea of the vanity of human wishes. The description of the broken statue of a cruel and powerful king gives the lines

> My name is Ozymandias, king of kings:
> Look on my works, ye Mighty, and despair!

tremendous force. The vain, proud king who thought he would be remembered and feared for ever is now nothing more than a 'colossal wreck' in the desert.

Each of the stanzas in *The Ancient Mariner* with the exception of the first is meant to bring home the idea that the ship is motionless: the sails drop down, the sun stands directly above the mast, and

> Day after day, day after day,
> We stuck, nor breath nor motion.

Turn back to the poems *Lucy*, *To a Poet a Thousand Years Hence*, and *On His Eighty-sixth Birthday* and see if you can find similar pictures. Explain their purpose in the poems.

Repetition. Poets often repeat single lines or whole stanzas at intervals to emphasize a particular idea. Repetition is to be found in poetry which is aiming at special musical effects or when a poet wants us to pay very close attention to something.

Note the repetition of the word 'water' in these lines from the *Ancient Mariner*:

> Water, water, everywhere,
> And all the boards did shrink;
> Water, water, everywhere
> Nor any drop to drink.

The poet makes us feel how vast the ocean is by repeating the word 'water' over and over again. At the same time he helps us to understand how thirsty the sailors are. For them, water is something that is everywhere and at the same moment nowhere.

In *On his Eighty-sixth Birthday* the last words in the first lines of each stanza are repeated: 'faith with me', 'since have said', and 'overmuch'. This gives the poem a fine musical quality and points to the subject-matter of each stanza. That the world has 'kept faith' with him is an important idea and is given twice. This links up with the promise in the last stanza: a promise which has not been broken because the poet listened attentively to the oft-repeated warning in the second stanza.

SENSE DEVICES

Simile, metaphor, personification. Simile and metaphor are very special devices indeed. Their peculiar effect lies in the way apparently unrelated objects or ideas are brought together. A poet often compels us to fix our attention on one object while comparing it with another. It may be said that the quality of a poet often depends on his ability to bring together objects and ideas which are unconnected.

Simile. This is a direct comparison and can be recognized by the use of the words *like* and *as*.

The most striking example of simile in the poems you have studied occurs in these lines from *The Ancient Mariner*:

> Day after day, day after day,
> We stuck, nor breath nor motion;
> *As* idle *as* a painted ship
> Upon a painted ocean.

By relating the real ship to a painted one, Coleridge enables us to imagine just how still the ship was. We immediately see it like a ship in the middle of a painted picture, unmoving, and unchanging, destined to stay in the same place for ever.

In the poem *Lucy*, Wordsworth compares the girl to a star:

> —Fair *as* a star, when only one
> Is shining in the sky.

By bringing together the girl and the star (and making it the very first star of the evening), the poet helps us to understand that Lucy had the sort of beauty one could easily fail to notice.

The poem *To a Poet a Thousand Years Hence* contains these lines:

> *Like* a wind
> That falls at eve our fancies blow.

Here the poet has deliberately chosen a common simile (he says himself it is three thousand years old) to convey the idea that over the course of thousands of years essentially the same conditions prevail no matter how much material progress man may make.

Metaphor. This is rather like a simile except that the comparison is not direct but implied: the words *like* and *as* are not used. The poet does not say that one object is *like* another; he says it *is* another.

In the poem *Lucy*, Wordsworth does not say that the girl was *like* a violet. He writes:

> A violet by a mossy stone
> Half hidden from the eye.

Lucy, in these lines, *is* a violet. The metaphor vividly expresses the basic idea of the poem: it represents a girl of rare beauty who 'lived unknown'. A violet half hidden by a stone is similarly something rare and beautiful which, for most people, 'lives unknown'.

The line 'the furrow followed free' from the *Ancient Mariner* is also a metaphor because a furrow, when taken literally is only to be found in a ploughed field. In this context it is used to describe the speed of the ship: it went so rapidly that it made a 'furrow' in the sea. Turn back to this poem and find another example of metaphor.

Shelley, in *Ozymandias*, compresses a great deal of meaning into the metaphor 'The hand that mocked them and the heart that fed.' Though on the surface he appears to be describing nothing more than a broken statue, he manages to combine with it a description of the character of the king who died long ago. From this line we can see that Ozymandias was cruel and showed contempt for his people ('the hand that mocked them'), while they, in turn, were at his mercy ('the heart that fed').

Explain the purpose of the following metaphors taken from the remaining poems you have read.

Cargoes:

'Butting through the Channel in the mad March days'.

To a Poet a Thousand Years Hence:

'sweet archaic song'.
'Send you my words for messengers
   The way I shall not pass along'.
'ride secure the cruel sky'.
'bright-eyed love'.

On his Eighty-sixth Birthday:

'. . . that mysterious voice you shed
From clouds and hills around'.
'they dropped underground'.
'neutral-tinted haps'.

Personification. This occurs when inanimate objects are given a human form, or when they are made to speak. There is only one instance of this device in the poems you have read and it is to be found in *On his Eighty-sixth Birthday*. The world 'speaks' these words:

Many have loved me desperately,
Many with smooth serenity,
While some have shown contempt of me
   Till they dropped underground.

By means of personification here the poet underlines the close relationship that existed between himself and the world.

SOUND DEVICES

Alliteration, onomatopoeia, rhyme, assonance, rhythm. These have difficult names but they are not as hard as they look. All of them add considerably to the musical quality a poem has when it is read aloud.

B

Alliteration. This is the repetition of the same sound at frequent intervals. One of the most obvious examples from the poems you have read occurs in *The Ancient Mariner*:

> The *f*air *b*reeze *b*lew, the white *f*oam *f*lew,
> The *f*urrow *f*ollowed *f*ree.

The repeated 'b's and 'f's here make the lines run quickly and give the impression of a ship travelling at high speed. Further on, the line

> *D*ay after *d*ay, *d*ay after *d*ay

with its repeated 'd' sound suggests both monotony and immobility.

Another good example of alliteration occurs in *Cargoes*:

> Dirty British *c*oaster with a *s*alt-*c*a*k*ed
> *s*mo*k*e-*st*a*ck*

The soft 's' and hard 'k' sounds add to the verbal description of the small and dirty coaster which is butting its way across the Channel and even further stress the grace and beauty of movement of the ships that went before.

Explain the effect of

> *b*oundless and *b*are
> The *l*one and *l*evel *s*ands *s*tretch far away.

from *Ozymandias* and find other examples in the same poem.

Onomatopoeia occurs in words which imitate sounds and thus suggest the object described: words like cuckoo, hum, buzz, swish, crash, jangle, etc. There are no striking instances of this device in the poems you have read but examples will be found in the poems given for study in Chapters 3 and 4.

Rhyme. This usually occurs at line endings in poetry and consists of words which have the same sound; the letters preceding the vowel, must, however, be unlike in sound. For instance: 'night' and 'sight' are true rhymes; 'night' and 'knight' or 'sight' and 'site' are not.

Skilful rhyming can be very effective indeed as we can

see from the stanzas from the *Ancient Mariner*. At the beginning of the poem there are not only rhymes at the end of each line, but *internal* rhymes as well, that is two rhyming words within a single line:

> The fair breeze *blew*, the white foam *flew*,
> The furrow followed *free*;
> We were the *first* that ever *burst*
> Into that silent *sea*.

So many rhymes in rapid succession quicken the pace of the poem. When the ship stops, Coleridge does not use internal rhymes and the pace becomes much slower:

> All in a hot and copper sky,
> The bloody Sun, at *noon*
> Right up above the mast did stand,
> No bigger than the *Moon*.

There are only two rhymes here as opposed to six in the previous stanza.

Poets handle rhymes with great care. If they are used too much a poem may be made monotonous. Notice how Masefield avoids monotony in *Cargoes* by using only two rhymes in each stanza: Palestine and wine, shores and moidores, days and trays.

Assonance. This occurs when a poet introduces imperfect rhymes: 'wreck' and 'rock', 'grind' and 'ground', 'speak' and 'break' etc. It is often employed deliberately to avoid the jingling sound of a too-insistent rhyme pattern.

In *To a Poet a Thousand Years Hence*, 'years' is made to rhyme with 'messengers', 'sky' with 'masonry' and 'wind' with 'blind'. In this way the rhymes do not fall into a sing-song pattern and the lines flow easily.

Find examples of assonance in *Ozymandias*, *Lucy* and the first stanza of *On his Eighty-sixth Birthday*, and explain how they help to vary the rhyme schemes used.

Rhythm. Poetry has much in common with music. When we read a poem aloud, it is nearly always possible to notice that the sounds used follow a definite pattern and are meant to appeal to the ear. This pattern of sounds which a poet imposes on the language he uses is called *rhythm* and it is the most striking of all sound devices.

A poem may be reduced to a meaningless jingle if the sound does not closely match the sense. The rhythm of a poem must always help to convey the poet's intention and give us some indication of his mood.

Notice how in the lines from *The Ancient Mariner* the rhythm of 'The fair breeze blew, the white foam flew' matches the speed of the ship. When the ship stops, the rhythm alters and the pace of the poem becomes much slower:

> Day after day, day after day,
> We stuck, nor breath nor motion;

Wordsworth does something similar in *Lucy*. The last lines of the first two stanzas ('And very few to love', 'Is shining in the sky') have the same rhythm. The last line of the final stanza ('The difference to me') is, however, a foot short and is deliberately meant to jar. It is discordant and at once conveys the poet's sorrow.

In *On his Eighty-sixth Birthday* Hardy maintains the same sound pattern throughout and the gentle rhythm emphasizes the poet's quiet resignation to life. The repetitions echo the rhythm of the opening lines of each stanza and slow down the pace of the poem.

3

TYPES

In the exercises that follow, the poems to be considered have been divided into groups to help you recognize some of the most common types of poetry: Descriptive, Reflective, Narrative, the Lyric, and the Sonnet. The ability to distinguish between these types, though not indispensable for appreciation, is important as it will help you to understand more readily what a poet's intentions are.

Descriptive

Poems which describe people or experiences, scenes or objects.

[1] *The Dead Crab*

A rosy shield upon its back,
That not the hardest storm could crack,
From whose sharp edge projected out
Black pin-point eyes staring about;
Beneath, the well-knit cote-armure   5
That gave to its weak belly power;
The clustered legs with plated joints
That ended in stiletto points;
The claws like mouths it held outside:—
I cannot think this creature died   10
By storm or fish or sea-fowl harmed
Walking the sea so heavily armed;
Or does it make for death to be
Oneself a living armoury?

ANDREW YOUNG

Vocabulary

cote-armure (l. 5): coat of mail, armour.
clustered (l. 7): gathered together in a bunch.
plated (l. 7): covered with a hard outer shell for protection.
stiletto (l. 8): dagger, a small, very sharp knife.

QUESTIONS

1. Give the general and detailed meaning of the poem and what you consider to be the poet's intention.

2. Is there anything in the poem to suggest that the poet may have had a knight in armour in mind when describing the crab?

3. What sort of device is to be found in the phrase 'claws like mouths'? (l. 9). What does the phrase suggest to you?

4. 'Black pin-point eyes' (l. 4), is a metaphor. Find two more metaphors and comment on them.

5. What makes the poet's description of the crab so vivid?

[2] *Winter*

When icicles hang by the wall,
 And Dick the shepherd blows his nail,
And Tom bears logs into the hall,
 And milk comes frozen home in pail,
When blood is nipp'd, and ways be foul, 5
Then nightly sings the staring owl,
   Tu-who;
Tu-whit, to-who—a merry note,
While greasy Joan doth keel the pot.

When all aloud the wind doth blow, 10
 And coughing drowns the parson's saw,
And birds sit brooding in the snow,
 And Marian's nose looks red and raw,
When roasted crabs hiss in the bowl,
Then nightly sings the staring owl, 15
   Tu-who;
Tu-whit, tu-who—a merry note,
While greasy Joan doth keel the pot.

      WILLIAM SHAKESPEARE

Vocabulary

blows his nail (l. 2): warms the ends of his fingers by breathing on them.

nipp'd (l. 5): sharply bitten (by the cold).

keel (l. 9): stir and skim.

saw (l. 11): good advice.

crabs (l. 14): wild apples.

QUESTIONS

1. Give the general and detailed meaning of the poem and what you consider to be the poet's intention.

2. What illustrations does Shakespeare use to make us feel that the weather is cold? How does he contrast cold and warmth?

3. What is the effect of the repetition at the end of each stanza?

4. What sort of device is to be found in these words: 'Tu-who' (l. 7) and 'hiss' (l. 14)?

5. Find one example of assonance in the poem.

[3] *There's Been a Death*

There's been a death in the opposite house
    As lately as today.
I know it by the numb look
    Such houses have alway.

The neighbours rustle in and out,   5
    The doctor drives away.
A window opens like a pod,
    Abrupt, mechanically;

Somebody flings a mattress out,—
    The children hurry by;   10
They wonder if It died on that,—
    I used to when a boy.

The minister goes stiffly in
    As if the house were his,
And he owned all the mourners now,   15
    And little boys besides;

And then the milliner, and the man
    Of the appalling trade,
To take the measure of the house.
    There'll be that dark parade   20

Of tassels and of coaches soon;
    It's easy as a sign,—
The intuition of the news
    In just a country town.

EMILY DICKINSON

Vocabulary

    pod (l. 7): the part of a plant that contains seeds when the
    flower has fallen.

    tassels (l. 21): number of threads fixed together and hanging
    from a cloth.

    intuition (l. 23): understanding by instinct or feeling, rather
    than by reason or direct evidence.

QUESTIONS

1. Give the general and detailed meaning of the poem and what
   you consider to be the poet's intention.

2. Find an example of illustration in this poem. What idea does
   it illustrate?

3. Why are the following words particularly well-chosen: rustle
   (l. 5); It (l. 11); stiffly (l. 13)?

4. Name the devices contained in the following words and phrases
   and say what they do: numb look (l. 3); like a pod (l. 7); As
   if the house were his/And he owned all the mourners now
   (ll. 14, 15); to take the measure of the house (l. 19).

5. Find three examples of assonance. In what way does assonance
   in this poem suit the subject-matter?

Reflective

Thoughtful poems often containing a great deal of description which the poet comments on or from which he

draws conclusions. Sometimes these conclusions are directly
stated; at other times implied.

[1] *The Dead*

These hearts were woven of human joys and cares,
  Washed marvellously with sorrow, swift to mirth.
The years had given them kindness. Dawn was theirs,
  And sunset, and the colours of the earth.
These had seen movement, and heard music; known   5
  Slumber and waking; loved; gone proudly friended;
Felt the quick stir of wonder; sat alone;
  Touched flowers and furs and cheeks. All this is ended.

There are waters blown by changing winds to laughter
And lit by the rich skies, all day. And after,   10
  Frost, with a gesture, stays the waves that dance
And wandering loveliness. He leaves a white
  Unbroken glory, a gathered radiance,
A width, a shining peace, under the night.

RUPERT BROOKE

QUESTIONS

1. Give the general and detailed meaning of the poem and what
   you consider to be the poet's intention.

2. Point out the contrast in the poem.

3. How does the poet show that there is a great deal of variety in
   life?

4. What are the poet's feelings about death?

5. In what way does the metaphor in the second stanza suit the
   subject-matter?

[2] *An Irish Airman Foresees his Death*

I know that I shall meet my fate
Somewhere among the clouds above;
Those that I fight I do not hate,
Those that I guard I do not love;
My country is Kiltartan Cross,   5

My countrymen Kiltartan's poor,
No likely end could bring them loss
Or leave them happier than before.
Nor law, nor duty bade me fight,
Nor public men, nor cheering crowds,   10
A lonely impulse of delight
Drove to this tumult in the clouds;
I balanced all, brought all to mind,
The years to come seemed waste of breath,
A waste of breath the years behind   15
In balance with this life, this death.

W. B. YEATS

QUESTIONS

1. Give the general and detailed meaning of the poem and what
   you consider to be the poet's intention.

2. In what senses is the airman 'above' war and politics?

3. What do we learn of the airman's character?

4. Name the devices contained in the following phrases and say
   what they do: 'waste of breath' (ll. 14, 15); 'In balance with
   this life, this death.' (l. 16).

[3] *Mild the Mist upon the Hill*

Mild the mist upon the hill,
    Telling not of storms tomorrow;
No; the day has wept its fill,
    Spent its store of silent sorrow.

Oh, I'm gone back to the days of youth,   5
    I am a child once more,
And 'neath my father's sheltering roof,
    And near the old hall door.

I watch this cloudy evening fall,
    After a day of rain: 10
Blue mists, sweet mists of summer pall
    The horizon's mountain-chain.

The damp stands in the long, green grass
    As thick as morning's tears;
And dreamy scents of fragrance pass   15
    That breathe of other years.

EMILY BRONTË

Vocabulary

'neath (l. 7): beneath.

pall (l. 11): a pall is a black or purple cloth which is spread over
a coffin. Here the word is used as a verb in the sense of 'cover'
or 'hide'.

QUESTIONS

1. Give the general and detailed meaning of the poem and what you consider to be the poet's intention.

2. Why is the poet reminded of the past?

3. What is the poet's mood?

4. Name the devices contained in the following lines and say what they do: '. . . the day has wept its fill, /Spent its store of silent sorrow.' (ll. 3–4); 'As thick as morning's tears;' (l. 14); '. . . dreamy scents of fragrance pass/ That breathe of other years.' (ll. 15–16). How do they help convey the poet's mood?

5. Find one example of assonance in the poem.

Narrative

Poems which tell a story. They tend to be longer than other types of poetry but it is comparatively easy to recognize the poet's intention.

[1] *Lord Randal*

'O where have you been, Lord Randal, my son?
O where have you been, my handsome young man?'—
    'I have been to the wild wood; mother, make my bed
      soon,
For I'm weary with hunting, and fain would lie down.'

'Who gave you your dinner, Lord Randal, my son?   5
Who gave you your dinner, my handsome young man?'—
  'I dined with my sweetheart; mother, make my bed
      soon,
For I'm weary with hunting, and fain would lie down.'

'What had you for dinner, Lord Randal, my son?
What had you for dinner, my handsome young man?'— 10
  'I had eels boiled in broth; mother, make my bed soon,
For I'm weary with hunting, and fain would lie down.'

'And where are your bloodhounds, Lord Randal, my
      son?
And where are your bloodhounds, my handsome young
      man?'—
  'O they swelled and they died; mother, make my bed
      soon,   15
For I'm weary with hunting, and fain would lie down.'

'O I fear you are poisoned, Lord Randal, my son!
O I fear you are poisoned, my handsome young man!'—
  'O yes! I am poisoned; mother, make my bed soon,
For I'm sick at the heart, and I fain would lie down.'

POET UNKNOWN

Vocabulary

soon . . . down: This is a Scottish poem and in Scots pronuncia-
    tion 'down' would be read 'doon' to rhyme with 'soon'.
fain (l. 4): I would like to.
eels (l. 11): snake-like fish.
broth (l. 11): thin soup.
bloodhounds (l. 13): hunting dogs.

QUESTIONS

1. Give the general and detailed meaning of the poem and what
   you consider to be the poet's intention.
2. Do you think the story in this poem is well told? What part
   does repetition play in the telling of it?

3. In what way is the last line of the poem meant to surprise us?
4. Discuss the rhythm and rhyme scheme of the poem.

[2] *Soliloquy of the Spanish Cloister*

Gr-r-r—there go, my heart's abhorrence!
Water your damned flower-pots, do!
If hate killed men, Brother Lawrence,
    God's blood, would not mine kill you!
What? your myrtle-bush wants trimming?   5
    Oh, that rose has prior claims—
Needs its leaden vase filled brimming?
    Hell dry you up with its flames!

At the meal we sit together:
    Salve tibi! I must hear   10
Wise talk of the kind of weather,
    Sort of season, time of year:
Not a plenteous cork-crop: scarcely
    Dare we hope oak-galls, I doubt:
What's the Latin name for 'parsley'?   15
    What's the Greek name for Swine's Snout?

Whew! We'll have our platter burnished,
    Laid with care on our own shelf!
With a fire-new spoon we're furnished,
    And a goblet for ourself,   20
Rinsed like something sacrificial
    Ere 'tis fit to touch our chaps—
Marked with L. for our initial!
    (He-he! There his lily snaps!)

Saint, forsooth! While brown Dolores   25
    Squats outside the Convent bank
With Sanchicha, telling stories,
    Steeping tresses in the tank,
Blue-black, lustrous, thick like horsehairs,
    —Can't I see his dead eye glow,   30
Bright as 'twere a Barbary corsair's?
    (That is, if he'd let it show!)

When he finishes refection,
    Knife and fork he never lays
Cross-wise, to my recollection,   35
    As do I, in Jesu's praise.
I the Trinity illustrate,
    Drinking watered orange-pulp—
In three sips the Arian frustrate;
    While he drains his at one gulp!   40

Oh, those melons? If he's able
    We're to have a feast! so nice!
One goes to the Abbot's table,
    All of us get each a slice.
How go on your flowers? None double?   45
    Not one fruit-sort can you spy?
Strange!—And I, too, at such trouble,
    Keep them close-nipped on the sly!

There's a great text in Galatians,
    Once you trip on it, entails   50
Twenty-nine distinct damnations,
    One sure, if another fails;
If I trip him just a-dying,
    Sure of heaven as sure can be,
Spin him round and send him flying   55
    Off to hell, a Manichee?

Or, my scrofulous French novel
    On grey paper with blunt type!
Simply glance at it, you grovel
    Hand and foot in Belial's gripe: 60
If I double down its pages
    At the woeful sixteenth print,
When he gathers his greengages,
    Ope a sieve and slip it in't?

Or, there's Satan!—One might venture   65
    Pledge one's soul to him, yet leave
Such a flaw in the indenture
    As he'd miss till, past retrieve,

Blasted lay that rose-acacia
   We're so proud of! *Hy, Zy, Hine* . . .   70
'St, there's Vespers! *Plena gratiâ*
   Ave, Virgo. Gr-r-r—you swine!

ROBERT BROWNING

Vocabulary

soliloquy: talking to oneself.

cloister: a covered and pillared walk enclosing a quadrangle in a monastery.

my heart's abhorrence (l. 1): i.e., you whom I hate with all my heart.

God's blood (l. 4): a curse.

has prior claims (l. 6): requires attention first.

needs its . . . (l. 7): i.e., 'does its leaden vase need . . .'

brimming (l. 7): full to the top.

salve tibi (l. 10): 'greetings'.

plenteous (l. 13): plentiful.

oak-gall(s) (l. 14): growth that is caused by insects on oak trees and used for making ink.

snout (l. 16): nose of an animal.

we'll have our platter burnished (l. 17): i.e. his (Brother Lawrence's) dish will be polished.

fire-new . . . furnished (l. 19): i.e., he is provided with a brand-new spoon.

ere (l. 22): before.

chaps (l. 22): jaws, lower half of the face.

forsooth (l. 25): indeed.

squats (l. 26): crouches in a half-sitting position.

steeping tresses (l. 28): washing her hair.

lustrous (l. 29): shining.

Barbary corsair's (l. 31): a pirate off the coast of N. Africa.

refection (l. 33): dinner.

the Arian frustrate (l. 39): defeat those who deny that the body and blood of Christ are actually present in the bread and wine taken at the Communion service.

drains . . . gulp (l. 40): swallows his greedily and all at once.

keep . . . sly (l. 48): i.e., I cut them off when you're not looking.

entails (l. 50): means that you will suffer, necessitates.

Manichee (l. 56): one who believes that Man was created by Satan in his own image and that demons and angels are continually at war for the possession of men's souls.

scrofulous (l. 57): diseased.

grovel . . . gripe (ll. 59–60): lie in the hands of the devil.

greengages (l. 63): kind of fruit.

ope (l. 64): open.

venture pledge (ll. 65–6): i.e., venture *to* pledge.

indenture (l. 67): contract.

Vespers (l. 71): evening prayers.

plena gratiâ (l. 71): 'full of grace'—part of a prayer.

Ave, Virgo (l. 72): 'hail, Mary'.

QUESTIONS

1. Give the general and detailed meaning of the poem and what you consider to be the poet's intention.

2. Write a brief character sketch of the monk who is telling the story.

3. Point out two illustrations and discuss their purpose.

4. Find three similes and two metaphors and say what they do.

5. In what way does the rhythm of the poem help to convey the poet's intentions?

[3] *The Destruction of Sennacherib*

The Assyrian came down like the wolf on the fold,
And his cohorts were gleaming in purple and gold;
And the sheen of their spears was like stars on the sea,
When the blue wave rolls nightly on deep Galilee.

Like the leaves of the forest when Summer is green,   5
That host with their banners at sunset were seen:
Like the leaves of the forest when Autumn hath blown,
That host on the morrow lay wither'd and strown.

For the Angel of Death spread his wings on the blast,
And breathed in the face of the foe as he pass'd;   10

And the eyes of the sleepers wax'd deadly and chill,
And their hearts but once heaved, and for ever grew still!

And there lay the steed with his nostril all wide,
But through it there roll'd not the breath of his pride;
And the foam of his gasping lay white on the turf,   15
And cold as the spray of the rock-beating surf.

And there lay the rider distorted and pale,
With the dew on his brow, and the rust on his mail,
And the tents were all silent, the banners alone,
The lances unlifted, the trumpet unblown.   20

And the widows of Ashur are loud in their wail,
And the idols are broke in the temple of Baal;
And the might of the Gentile, unsmote by the sword,
Hath melted like snow in the glance of the Lord!

GEORGE GORDON, LORD BYRON

Vocabulary

> fold (l. 1): enclosure in which sheep are kept.
> cohorts (l. 2): bands of soldiers.
> sheen (l. 3): brightness.
> host (l. 6): army.
> banners (l. 6): flags carried in war.
> strown (l. 8): past participle of 'strew', scattered.
> wax'd (l. 11): became, grew.
> steed (l. 13): horse.
> lances (l. 20): long wooden weapons with pointed steel tips.
> unsmote (l. 23): not struck.

QUESTIONS

1. Give the general and detailed meaning of the poem and what you consider to be the poet's intention.

2. Discuss the effectiveness of two of the illustrations used to describe defeat in battle.

3. What devices are used in the second stanza? Describe their purpose.

4. Find two metaphors and two examples of alliteration in the poem and say what they do.

The Lyric

A short poem like a song which is usually the expression of a mood or feeling.

[1] *Full Fathom Five*

Full fathom five thy father lies;
　Of his bones are coral made:
Those are pearls that were his eyes:
　Nothing of him that doth fade,
But doth suffer a sea-change　　　　　　5
Into something rich and strange.
Sea-nymphs hourly ring his knell:
　Hark! now I hear them,—
　　Ding-dong, bell.

WILLIAM SHAKESPEARE

Vocabulary

fathom (l. 1): measure of six feet, used when calculating the depth of water.
sea-nymphs (l. 7): mermaids.
knell (l. 7): death-bell.
hark (l. 8): listen.

QUESTIONS

1. Give the general and detailed meaning of the poem and what you consider to be the poet's intention.
2. Find examples of each of the following and describe their effect: (a) metaphor, (b) alliteration, (c) onomatopoeia.

[2] *To —*

Music, when soft voices die,
Vibrates in the memory—
Odours, when sweet violets sicken,
Live within the sense they quicken.

Rose leaves, when the rose is dead,   5
Are heaped for the belovèd's bed;
And so thy thoughts, when thou art gone,
Love itself shall slumber on.

PERCY BYSSHE SHELLEY

Vocabulary

quicken (l. 4): bring to life.

QUESTIONS

1. Give the general and detailed meaning of the poem and what you consider to be the poet's intention.
2. Discuss the importance of metaphor in this poem.
3. In what way does the rhythm of this poem match its meaning?

[3] *Blow, Bugle, Blow*

The splendour falls on castle walls
    And snowy summits old in story:
The long light shakes across the lakes,
    And the wild cataract leaps in glory.
Blow, bugle, blow, set the wild echoes flying,   5
Blow, bugle; answer, echoes, dying, dying, dying.

O hark, O hear! how thin and clear,
    And thinner, clearer, farther going!
O sweet and far from cliff and scar
    The horns of Elfland faintly blowing!   10
Blow, let us hear the purple glens replying:
Blow, bugle; answer, echoes, dying, dying, dying.

O love, they die in yon rich sky,
    They faint on hill or field or river:
Our echoes roll from soul to soul,   15
    And grow for ever and for ever.
Blow, bugle, blow, set the wild echoes flying,
And answer, echoes, answer, dying, dying, dying.

ALFRED, LORD TENNYSON

Vocabulary

cataract (l. 4): waterfall.
bugle (l. 5): musical instrument resembling a small trumpet.
scar (l. 9): the steep part of a rocky mountain side.
Elfland (l. 10): fairy-land.
glens (l. 11): valleys.
yon (l. 13): yonder, the distant.

QUESTIONS

1. Give the general and detailed meaning of the poem and what you consider to be the poet's intention.
2. Discuss the importance of alliteration and onomatopoeia in this poem.

The Sonnet

A poem of fourteen lines which follows a very strict rhyme pattern. It is usually divided into two parts: the 'octave' (the first eight lines), and the 'sestet' (the last six lines). The octave and sestet are separated by a break in thought: a general statement made in the octave is illustrated or amplified in the sestet. Sonnets tend to be difficult because a great deal of meaning is often conveyed in a few lines.

There are three main types of Sonnet: the *Petrarchan*, the *Shakespearean* and the *Miltonic*.

THE PETRARCHAN SONNET

This is the strictest of the three types since only two rhymes are permitted in the octave and not more than three in the sestet. The octave is rhymed *a-b-b-a-a-b-b-a* and the sestet *c-d-e-c-d-e* (if three rhymes are used) and *c-d-c-d-c-d* (if two rhymes are used).

[1] On the Grasshopper and Cricket

The poetry of earth is never dead:	a
When all the birds are faint with the hot sun,	b
And hide in cooling trees, a voice will run	b

From hedge to hedge about the new-mown mead;   a
That is the Grasshopper's—he takes the lead   5 a
  In summer luxury,—he has never done   b
  With his delights; for when tired out with fun   b
He rests at ease beneath some pleasant weed.   a

The poetry of earth is ceasing never: c
  On a lone winter evening, when the frost   10 d
Has wrought a silence, from the stove there shrills   e
The Cricket's song, in warmth increasing ever,   c
  And seems to one in drowsiness half-lost,   d
The Grasshopper's among some grassy hills.   e

JOHN KEATS

Vocabulary

  mead (l. 4): meadow, field.
  done (l. 6): finished.
  wrought (l. 11): made, created.
  drowsiness (l. 13): sleepiness.

QUESTIONS

1. Give the general and detailed meaning of the poem and what you consider to be the poet's intention.
2. In what way does the sestet differ from the octave?
3. What is the main contrast drawn in the poem?
4. Discuss the effectiveness of two metaphors in the poem.

THE SHAKESPEAREAN SONNET

Though this type of sonnet is also divided into octave and sestet, it has a much simpler rhyme pattern. It is really a poem consisting of three stanzas each of four lines in length (these are called 'quatrains'). The sonnet ends with two rhyming lines, called 'a rhyming couplet'. The pattern is as follows: *a-b-a-b-c-d-c-d-e-f-e-f-g-g*.

[2] *Time*

Like as the waves make towards the pebbled shore,   a
So do our minutes hasten to their end;   b

Each changing place with that which goes before,   a
In sequent toil all forwards do contend.   b
Nativity, once in the main of light,   5 c
Crawls to maturity, wherewith being crown'd,   d
Crooked eclipses 'gainst his glory fight,   c
And Time that gave, doth now his gift confound.   d
Time doth transfix the flourish set on youth,   e
And delves the parallels in beauty's brow;   10 f
Feeds on the rarities of nature's truth,   e
And nothing stands but for his scythe to mow: f
And yet to times in hope my verse shall stand,   g
Praising thy worth, despite his cruel hand.   g

WILLIAM SHAKESPEARE

Vocabulary

sequent (l. 4): one following the other.
all forwards do contend (l. 4): are always striving to move onward.
wherewith (l. 6): with which.
transfix the flourish set on (l. 9): destroy the outward attraction.
delves the parallels (l. 10): digs lines.
scythe (l. 12): long curved blade used for cutting grass. Time when personified is often pictured as a reaper with a scythe.

QUESTIONS

1. Give the general and detailed meaning of the poem and what you consider to be the poet's intention.

2. How does the sestet differ from the octave?

3. Comment on the importance of simile and metaphor in the poem.

THE MILTONIC SONNET

This has the same rhyme scheme as the Petrarchan sonnet but differs in one important respect: there is no break in thought between the octave and sestet.

[3] *On His Blindness*

When I consider how my light is spent,	a
Ere half my days, in this dark world and wide,	b
And that one Talent which is death to hide	b
Lodg'd with me useless, though my Soul more bent	a
To serve therewith my Maker, and present 5	a
My true account, lest he returning chide,	b
Doth God exact day-labour, light deny'd,	b
I fondly ask; But Patience, to prevent	a
That murmur, soon replies, God doth not need	c
Either man's work or his own gifts, who best 10	d
Bear his mild yoke, they serve him best, his State	e
Is Kingly. Thousands at his bidding speed	c
And post o'er Land and Ocean without rest:	d
They also serve who only stand and wait.	e

JOHN MILTON

Vocabulary

> spent (l. 1): used up.
> lodged (l. 4): remaining.
> bent (l. 4): inclined.
> therewith (l. 5): with this.
> chide (l. 6): rebuke, scold.
> exact (l. 7): demand.
> yoke (l. 11): burden.
> bidding (l. 12): command.
> post (l. 13): travel hastily.
> o'er (l. 13): over.

QUESTIONS

1. Give the general and detailed meaning of the poem and what you consider to be the poet's intention.

2. Show how the poet develops a single theme throughout the sonnet.

3. What examples are there of (a) metaphor, (b) personification in this poem and what do they do?

4

LITERARY APPRECIATION

Up to now you have learned how to find the meaning of a poem and recognize various devices. When you attempt full literary appreciation, what you write must be in continuous prose and clearly divided into paragraphs. It is not enough to spot devices: in each case you must say how a particular device is suited to the subject-matter of the poem. Never make a comment on a poem without proving it by referring to the text. It is hardly necessary to state that a single poem will not contain *every* type of device there is: it is up to you to find exactly what devices are employed.

The substance of the previous chapters is briefly re-stated here so that you may have a clear picture of what you have to do:

KEY

1. READING	Read carefully; look for a simple meaning.
2. MEANING	*General*
	Detailed: do *not* paraphrase.
	Intention

3. DEVICES

(a) STRUCTURAL	*Contrast*
	Illustration
	Repetition
(b) SENSE	*Simile*
	Metaphor
	Personification

(c) SOUND   *Alliteration*
                     Onomatopoeia
                     Rhyme
                     Assonance
                     Rhythm

Before beginning to write your appreciation, try and decide in your own mind what type of poem it is you are reading. This will help you discern the poet's intentions easily. The types you have studied are: descriptive, reflective, narrative, the lyric, and the sonnet.

Now carefully read and study this appreciation of the poem *Cargoes* which you read in Chapter I. Your own written appreciation of the poems that follow should be along these lines.

In this poem Masefield describes the various cargoes that have been carried by ships in three different ages.

The poet begins by describing two of the biggest and most beautiful ships of the past. The earlier of the two ships is a quinquireme; the later a 'stately Spanish galleon'. Both are pictured in bright sunshine carrying goods which, though different in kind, were both rare and precious. The quinquireme comes laden with ivory, strange animals and fine wood; the galleon with precious stones. The ship described in the last stanza is quite different. It belongs to modern times and is small ('a coaster') and dirty. It is on a short journey across the English Channel in bad weather with its cheap and useful cargo of coal, metal, and firewood.

The poet does not simply set out to describe cargoes but to make us consider how the present differs from the past. In the past the goods that were highly prized were beautiful, rare, and comparatively useless; in the present the goods are ugly, common and useful. From the way the poet describes these three different ships, we can see that he implies that modern times are less beautiful than former times.

This implication is achieved by means of contrast. The poet does not comment on the ages he writes about, but simply presents us with three different pictures. The first two of these are very similar and contrast strongly with the last. The ships of the past are among the finest of their kind. Both of them move through sunlit waters with their precious cargoes: the first to 'sunny Palestine', the second 'Through the Tropics by the palm-green shores'. By contrast, the 'British coaster' is a small and dirty vessel journeying across the Channel in late winter.

This contrast is vividly brought home by the choice of words. In the first two stanzas, the graceful movement of the ships is emphasized by the words 'rowing' and 'dipping'. The alliteration of '*s*andalwood, *c*edarwood', the choice of rare words like 'amethysts', 'topazes', and 'moidores' conveys the splendour of their cargoes. In the last stanza alliteration is again used but this time to produce entirely different effects. The repeated soft '*s*' and hard '*k*' sounds of '*c*oa*s*ter with a *s*alt-*c*a*k*ed *s*mo*k*e *s*tack' indicate that the ship is moving clumsily across the water. This point is clearly brought out by the metaphor in the next line: 'Butting through the Channel in the mad March days'. The ugly objects the ship is carrying have ugly names: 'coal, road-rail, pig-lead', and 'tin trays'. By using words like this the poet is indirectly commenting on our times. The cheap, mass-produced articles we value are useful but we have had to sacrifice a great deal of beauty to obtain them.

The limited use of rhymes (only two in each stanza) prevents the poet's description from becoming monotonous. Each part of the poem is beautifully balanced and follows the same pattern, reaching a climax in the last line of each stanza: 'Sandalwood, cedarwood . . .', 'Topazes, and cinnamon . . .', 'Firewood, ironware . . .' Emphasis on this line especially helps to convey the contrast the poet has been aiming at: the striking difference between the past and the present.

Write an appreciation of each of the following poems.

[1]

I must down to the seas again, to the lonely sea and the sky,
And all I ask is a tall ship and a star to steer her by,
And the wheel's kick and the wind's song and the white
      sail's shaking,
And a grey mist on the sea's face and a grey dawn
      breaking.

I must down to the seas again, for the call of the
      running tide   5
Is a wild call and a clear call that may not be denied;
And all I ask is a windy day with the white clouds flying,
And the flung spray and the blown spume, and the sea-
      gulls crying.

I must down to the seas again, to the vagrant gypsy
      life,
To the gull's way and the whale's way where the wind's
      like a whetted knife;   10
And all I ask is a merry yarn from a laughing fellow-rover,
And quiet sleep and a sweet dream when the long trick 's
      over.

                                                    JOHN MASEFIELD

Vocabulary
    spume (l. 8): foam.
    vagrant (l. 9): wandering.
    whetted (l. 10): sharpened.
    yarn (l. 11): tale.
    trick (l. 12): has two meanings here: (a) life; (b) a turn of duty
    at the ship's wheel.

[2]

Happy the man, whose wish and care
    A few paternal acres bound,
Content to breathe his native air
            In his own ground.

Whose herds with milk, whose fields with bread,   5
   Whose flocks supply him with attire;
Whose trees in summer yield him shade,
      In winter fire.

Blest, who can unconcern'dly find
   Hours, days, and years, slide soft away,   10
In health of body, peace of mind,
      Quiet by day.

Sound sleep by night; study and ease,
   Together mixed; sweet recreation:
And innocence, which most does please   15
      With meditation.

Thus let me live, unseen, unknown,
   Thus unlamented let me die,
Steal from the world, and not a stone
      Tell where I lie.

ALEXANDER POPE

Vocabulary

   acres (l. 2): a measure of land.
   attire (l. 6): dress.
   meditation (l. 16): thinking.
   unlamented (l. 18): without anyone weeping for me.
   steal (l. 19): go away quietly.

[3]

I wandered lonely as a cloud
That floats on high o'er vales and hills,
When all at once I saw a crowd,
A host of golden daffodils;
Beside the lake, beneath the trees,   5
Fluttering and dancing in the breeze.

Continuous as the stars that shine
And twinkle on the milky way,
They stretched in never-ending line
Along the margin of a bay: 10

Ten thousand saw I at a glance
Tossing their heads in sprightly dance.

The waves beside them danced; but they
Out-did the sparkling waves in glee:
A poet could not but be gay,   15
In such a jocund company:
I gazed—and gazed—but little thought
What wealth the show to me had brought:

For oft, when on my couch I lie
In vacant or in pensive mood,   20
They flash upon that inward eye
Which is the bliss of solitude;
And then my heart with pleasure fills,
And dances with the daffodils.

WILLIAM WORDSWORTH

Vocabulary

o'er (l. 2): over.
vales (l. 2): valleys.
host (l. 4): large number of.
the milky way (l. 8): the galaxy; bright band of stars in the sky.
sprightly (l. 12): lively.
out-did (l. 14): were better than; surpassed.
in glee (l. 14): gaily.
could not but be (l. 15): could not do anything else except . . .
jocund (l. 16): merry.
oft (l. 19): often.
vacant (l. 20): mentally inactive.
pensive (l. 20): thoughtful.

[4]

Fair daffodils, we weep to see
You haste away so soon:
As yet the early-rising Sun
Has not attain'd his noon.
Stay, stay,   5

Until the hasting day
Has run
But to the evensong;
And, having pray'd together, we
Will go with you along.   10

We have short time to stay, as you,
We have as short a Spring;
As quick a growth to meet decay
As you, or any thing.
We die,   15
As your hours do, and dry
Away,
Like to the Summer's rain;
Or as the pearls of morning's dew
Ne'er to be found again.

ROBERT HERRICK

Vocabulary

evensong (l. 8): evening prayer in the Church of England.
go with you along (l. 10): i.e., go along with you.
ne'er (l. 20): never.

[5]

The grey sea and the long black land;
And the yellow half-moon large and low;
And the startled little waves that leap
In fiery ringlets from their sleep,
As I gain the cove with pushing prow,   5
And quench its speed i' the slushy sand.

Then a mile of warm sea-scented beach;
Three fields to cross till a farm appears;
A tap at the pane, the quick sharp scratch
And blue spurt of a lighted match,   10
And a voice less loud, thro' its joys and fears,
Than the two hearts beating each to each!

ROBERT BROWNING

Vocabulary

cove (l. 5): small bay.

and quench (l. 6): to put out a fire, or satisfy one's thirst; here
it has the sense of 'stop'.

slushy (l. 6): very soft and watery.

pane (l. 9): one of the panels of glass in a window.

[6]

Does the road wind uphill all the way?
   Yes, to the very end.
Will the day's journey take the whole long day?
   From morn to night, my friend.

But is there for the night a resting-place?   5
   A roof for when the slow dark hours begin.
May not the darkness hide it from my face?
   You cannot miss that inn.

Shall I meet other wayfarers at night?
   Those who have gone before.   10
Then must I knock, or call when just in sight?
   They will not keep you waiting at that door.

Shall I find comfort, travel-sore and weak?
   Of labour you shall find the sum.
Will there be beds for me and all who seek?   15
   Yea, beds for all who come.

CHRISTINA ROSSETTI

Vocabulary

wayfarers (l. 9): travellers.

[7]

Let me go where'er I will
I hear a sky-born music still:
It sounds from all things old,
It sounds from all things young,
From all that's fair, from all that's foul,   5
Peals out a cheerful song.
It is not only in the rose,

It is not only in the bird,
Nor only where the rainbow glows,
Nor in the song of woman heard,   10
But in the darkest, meanest things
There alway, alway something sings.
'Tis not in the high stars alone,
Nor in the cups of budding flowers,
Nor in the redbreast's mellow tone,   15
Nor in the bow that smiles in showers,
But in the mud and scum of things
There alway, alway something sings.

                         RALPH WALDO EMERSON

Vocabulary

peals out (l. 6): makes a loud and joyful ringing sound.
mellow (l. 15): rich and pure.
bow (l. 16): i.e., rainbow.
scum (l. 17): filth, dirt which comes to the surface as distinct
   from mud which does not.

[8] *Upon Westminster Bridge*

Earth has not anything to show more fair:
Dull would he be of soul who could pass by
A sight so touching in its majesty:
This City now doth, like a garment, wear
The beauty of the morning; silent, bare,   5
Ships, towers, domes, theatres, and temples lie
Open unto the fields, and to the sky;
All bright and glittering in the smokeless air.
Never did sun more beautifully steep
In his first splendour, valley, rock, or hill;   10
Ne'er saw I, never felt, a calm so deep!
The river glideth at his own sweet will:
Dear God! the very houses seem asleep;
And all that mighty heart is lying still!

                         WILLIAM WORDSWORTH

Vocabulary

steep (l. 9): bathe, pervade.

[9]

Slow, slow, fresh fount, keep time with my salt tears;
  Yet slower, yet, O faintly gentle springs;
List to the heavy part the music bears,
  Woe weeps out her division, when she sings.
      Droop herbs, and flowers;   5
      Fall grief in showers;
      Our beauties are not ours:
          O, I could still
(Like melting snow upon some craggy hill,)
          drop, drop, drop, drop,   10
Since nature's pride is, now, a wither'd daffodil.

                                    BEN JONSON

Vocabulary

  fount (l. 1): fountain.
  list (l. 3): listen.
  woe (l. 4): sorrow.
  herbs (l. 5): plants.
  wither'd (l. 11): dried-up.

[10]

Tiger! Tiger! burning bright
In the forests of the night,
What immortal hand or eye
Could frame thy fearful symmetry?

In what distant deeps or skies   5
Burnt the fire of thine eyes?
On what wings dare he aspire?
What the hand dare seize the fire?

And what shoulder, and what art,
Could twist the sinews of thy heart?   10
And when thy heart began to beat,
What dread hand? and what dread feet?

What the hammer? what the chain?
In what furnace was thy brain?

C

What the anvil? what dread grasp   15
Dare its deadly terrors clasp?

When the stars threw down their spears,
And water'd heaven with their tears,
Did he smile his work to see?
Did he who made the Lamb make thee?   20

Tiger! Tiger! burning bright
In the forests of the night,
What immortal hand or eye,
Dare frame thy fearful symmetry?

WILLIAM BLAKE

Vocabulary

frame (l. 4): shape.
symmetry (l. 4): well-proportioned body.
deeps (l. 5): deep parts of the sea.
what the hand (l. 8): i.e., which was the hand that . . .
sinews (l. 10): tendons (cords which work parts of the body).
furnace (l. 14): very hot fire in which metals are heated.
anvil (l. 15): block of iron on which metal is hammered.

[11]

Death, be not proud, though some have callèd thee
Mighty and dreadful, for thou art not so;
For those whom thou think'st thou dost overthrow
Die not, poor Death, nor yet canst thou kill me.
From Rest and Sleep, which but thy pictures be,   5
Much pleasure, then from thee much more must flow,
And soonest our best men with thee do go,
Rest of their bones and souls' delivery.
Thou art slave to fate, chance, kings, and desperate men,
And dost with poison, war, and sickness dwell;   10
And poppy or charms can make us sleep as well,
And better than thy stroke. Why swell'st thou then?
One short sleep past, we wake eternally,
And Death shall be no more: Death, thou shalt die!

JOHN DONNE

Vocabulary

for those . . . overthrow (l. 3): i.e., those whom you think you
     overthrow.
canst (l. 4): can.
dost (l. 10): do.
poppy (l. 11): in this sense 'opium'.
charms (l. 11): words or acts which have magic power.
swell'st thou (l. 12): i.e. why do you swell (with pride).
shalt (l. 14): shall.

[12]

'Is there anybody there?' said the Traveller,
     Knocking on the moonlit door;
And his horse in the silence champed the grasses
     Of the forest's ferny floor:
And a bird flew up out of the turret,   5
     Above the Traveller's head:
And he smote upon the door again a second time;
     'Is there anybody there?' he said.
But no one descended to the Traveller;
     No head from the leaf-fringed sill   10
Leaned over and looked into his grey eyes,
     Where he stood perplexed and still.
But only a host of phantom listeners
     That dwelt in the lone house then
Stood listening in the quiet of the moonlight   15
     To that voice from the world of men:
Stood thronging the faint moonbeams on the dark stair,
     That goes down to the empty hall,
Hearkening in an air stirred and shaken
     By the lonely Traveller's call.   20
And he felt in his heart their strangeness,
     Their stillness answering his cry,
While his horse moved, cropping the dark turf,
     'Neath the starred and leafy sky;
For he suddenly smote on the door, even   25
     Louder, and lifted his head:—

'Tell them I came, and no one answered,
   That I kept my word,' he said.
Never the least stir made the listeners,
   Though every word he spake   30
Fell echoing through the shadowiness of the still house
   From the one man left awake:
Ay, they heard his foot upon the stirrup,
   And the sound of iron on stone,
And how the silence surged softly backward,   35
   When the plunging hoofs were gone.

WALTER DE LA MARE

Vocabulary

   champed (l. 3): bit noisily.
   ferny (l. 4): covered with fern, a plant with feather-like leaves.
   turret (l. 5): small tower.
   smote (l. 7): past of 'smite'; struck.
   leaf-fringed sill (l. 10): the base of the window from which
      leaves were hanging loosely.
   host (l. 13): great number of.
   phantom (l. 13): ghostly.
   dwelt (l. 14): lived.
   thronging (l. 17): crowding in on each other.
   hearkening (l. 19): listening.
   cropping (l. 23): biting.
   turf (l. 23): grass.
   'neath (l. 24): i.e., beneath.
   spake (l. 30): i.e., spoke.
   ay (l. 33): yes.
   stirrup (l. 33): the foot-rest which hangs from the saddle.

[13]

   Tree at my window, window tree,
   My sash is lowered when night comes on;
   But let there never be curtain drawn
   Between you and me.

Vague dream-head lifted out of the ground,   5
And thing next most diffuse to cloud,
Not all your light tongues talking aloud
Could be profound.

But tree, I have seen you taken and tossed,
And if you have seen me when I slept,   10
You have seen me when I was taken and swept
And all but lost.

That day she put our heads together,
Fate had her imagination about her,
Your head so much concerned with outer,   15
Mine with inner, weather.

ROBERT FROST

Vocabulary

    sash (l. 2): a sash window has a top half and a bottom half
      each of which can be moved up or down.
    diffuse (l. 6): lacking a clearly defined outline.
    tossed (l. 9): thrown, shaken by the wind.

[14]

Look, stranger, at this island now
The leaping light for your delight discovers,
Stand stable here
And silent be,
That through the channels of the ear   5
May wander like a river
The swaying sound of the sea.

Here at the small field's ending pause
Where the chalk wall falls to the foam, and its tall ledges
Oppose the pluck   10
And knock of the tide,
And the shingle scrambles after the suck-
ing surf, and the gull lodges
A moment on its sheer side.

Far off like floating seeds the ships   15
Diverge on urgent voluntary errands;
And the full view
Indeed may enter
And move in memory as now these clouds do,
That pass the harbour mirror   20
And all the summer through the water saunter.

W. H. AUDEN

Vocabulary

ledges (l. 9): shelves on the side of the cliff.
pluck (l. 10): the pull exerted by the tide as it goes out.
shingle (l. 12): small stones; pebbles on the shore.
surf (l. 13): foam and movement of breaking waves.
lodges (l. 13): rests.
sheer (l. 14): so steep as to be perpendicular.
diverge (l. 16): move in different directions.
saunter (l. 21): walk very slowly.

[15]

Heaven-Haven

A NUN TAKES THE VEIL

I have desired to go
     Where springs not fail,
To fields where flies no sharp and sided hail,
     And a few lilies blow.

And I have asked to be   5
     Where no storms come,
Where the green swell is in the havens dumb,
     And out of the swing of the sea.

GERARD MANLEY HOPKINS

Vocabulary

sided (l. 3): which has sharp edges.
havens (l. 7): harbours.

[16]

The wind began to rock the grass
With threatening tunes and low,—
He threw a menace at the earth,
A menace at the sky.

The leaves unhooked themselves from trees   5
And started all abroad;
The dust did scoop itself like hands
And threw away the road.

The wagons quickened on the streets,
The thunder hurried slow;   10
The lightning showed a yellow beak,
And then a livid claw.

The birds put up the bars to nests,
The cattle fled to barns;
There came one drop of giant rain,   15
And then, as if the hands

That held the dams had parted hold,
The waters wrecked the sky,
But overlooked my father's house,
Just quartering a tree.

EMILY DICKINSON

Vocabulary

menace (l. 3): threat.
and started all abroad (l. 6): began flying in all directions.
livid (l. 12): blue-grey colour, like lead.
put up the bars (l. 13): barred and bolted (the 'doors' to their
    nests).
parted hold (l. 17): let go of each other.
overlooked (l. 19): in this sense, passed by and did not damage.
quartering (l. 20): here relates to 'the waters' and may be
    taken to mean 'splintering', 'shattering'.

[17]

Calm was the evening, as if asleep,
But sickled on high with brooding storm,
Couched in invisible space. And, lo!
I saw in utter silence sweep
Out of that darkening starless vault   5
A gliding spark, as blanched as snow,
That burned into dust, and vanished in
A hay-cropped meadow, brightly green.

A meteor from the cold of space,
Lost in Earth's wilderness of air?—   10
Presage of lightnings soon to shine
In splendour on this lonely place?—
I cannot tell; but only how fair
It glowed within the crystalline
Pure heavens, and of its strangeness lit   15
My mind to joy at sight of it.

Yet what is common as lovely may be:
The petalled daisy, a honey bell,
A pebble, a branch of moss, a gem
Of dew, or fallen rain—if we   20
A moment in their beauty dwell;
Entranced, alone, see only them.
How blind to wait, till, merely unique,
Some omen thus the all bespeak!

WALTER DE LA MARE

Vocabulary

sickled (l. 2): in this sense, 'threatened'. (A 'sickle' is a curved
   blade fitted into a short wooden handle and is used for cutting
   grass.)
brooding (l. 2): which was hanging over.
couched (l. 3): lying in wait.
vault (l. 5): arched roof, the heavens.
blanched (l. 6): white.
presage (l. 11): forewarning.
crystalline (l. 14): clear as crystal.

some omen ... bespeak (l. 24): some sign tells us about
   everything.

[18]

Let me not to the marriage of true minds
Admit impediments. Love is not love
Which alters when it alteration finds,
Or bends with the remover to remove:
O, no! it is an ever-fixèd mark,   5
That looks on tempests and is never shaken;
It is the star to every wandering bark,
Whose worth's unknown, although his height be taken.

Love's not Time's fool, though rosy lips and cheeks
Within his bending sickle's compass come;   10
Love alters not with his brief hours and weeks,
But bears it out ev'n to the edge of doom.
If this be error, and upon me prov'd,
I never writ, nor no man ever lov'd.

WILLIAM SHAKESPEARE

Vocabulary

   impediments (l. 2): things which hinder.
   bends with the remover to remove (l. 4): helps with its own
      removal.
   bark (l. 7): ship.
   within ... come (l. 10): come within the range (compass) of
      his sickle (curved blade used for cutting corn).
   writ (l. 14): wrote.

[19]

O what is that sound which so thrills the ear
   Down in the valley drumming, drumming?
Only the scarlet soldiers, dear,
   The soldiers coming.

O what is that light I see flashing so clear   5
   Over the distance brightly, brightly?
Only the sun on their weapons, dear,
   As they step lightly.

O what are they doing with all that gear;
  What are they doing this morning, this morning?   10
Only the usual manœuvres, dear,
  Or perhaps a warning.

O why have they left the road down there;
  Why are they suddenly wheeling, wheeling?
Perhaps a change in the orders, dear;   15
  Why are you kneeling?

O haven't they stopped for the doctor's care;
  Haven't they reined their horses, their horses?
Why, they are none of them wounded, dear,
  None of these forces.   20

O is it the parson they want with white hair;
  Is it the parson, is it, is it?
No, they are passing his gateway, dear,
  Without a visit.

O it must be the farmer who lives so near;   25
  It must be the farmer so cunning, so cunning?
They have passed the farm already, dear,
  And now they are running.

O where are you going? stay with me here!
  Were the vows you swore me deceiving, deceiving?   30
No, I promised to love you, dear,
  But I must be leaving.

O it's broken the lock and splintered the door,
  O it's the gate where they're turning, turning;
Their feet are heavy on the floor   35
  And their eyes are burning.

W. H. AUDEN

Vocabulary

  gear (l. 9): equipment.
  manœuvres (l. 11): military exercises.
  wheeling (l. 14): turning in formation.

[20]

The trees are in their autumn beauty,
The woodland paths are dry,
Under the October twilight the water
Mirrors a still sky;
Upon the brimming water among the stones   5
Are nine-and-fifty swans.

The nineteenth autumn has come upon me
Since I first made my count;
I saw, before I had well finished,
All suddenly mount   10
And scatter wheeling in great broken rings
Upon their clamorous wings.

I have looked upon those brilliant creatures,
And now my heart is sore.
All's changed since I, hearing at twilight,   15
The first time on this shore,
The bell-beat of their wings above my head,
Trod with a lighter tread.

Unwearied still, lover by lover,
They paddle in the cold   20
Companionable streams or climb the air;
Their hearts have not grown old;
Passion or conquest, wander where they will,
Attend upon them still.

But now they drift on the still water,   25
Mysterious, beautiful;
Among what rushes will they build,
By what lake's edge or pool
Delight men's eyes when I awake some day
To find they have flown away?

W. B. YEATS

Vocabulary

brimming (l. 5): very full; i.e., there is so much water that it
almost overflows its banks.

wheeling (l. 11): swinging round in a circle.

clamorous (l. 12): noisy; i.e., noise caused by the beating of the wings.

sore (l. 14): full of pain.

trod (l. 18): past tense of 'tread'; walked.

unwearied (l. 19): who have never got tired.

drift (l. 25): they are carried by the water.

rushes (l. 27): plants with long stems that grow near water.

Part II

PROSE

5

TYPES

We have seen that it is often possible to enjoy poetry without understanding its meaning. That is, you may pay rather closer attention to the music of a poem than to *what* it actually says. In prose, however, there is no rhyme and metre to obscure the meaning. A writer may express himself more directly because he does not have to make the language he uses fit a rigid pattern. Thus we read prose primarily for its meaning. Just as with poetry, enjoyment of prose is often directly related to the way a writer expresses himself; but no matter how pleasurable the way of writing may be, meaning always comes first.

The word 'prose' is used to define any sort of writing that does not fit a recognized poetical form. But not all prose is alike: there is almost endless variety in the way we express ourselves in writing. We should hardly expect a novel to be written in legal terms, or a scientific text-book to contain lengthy descriptions of the countryside. In each case, *style*, the way something has been written, must be adapted to suit the subject-matter.

Read the three short passages of prose that follow and try to explain in what ways they differ.

[1]

They were moving in upon him quickly, groping, yet moving rapidly. It was like playing blind man's buff, with everyone blindfolded except one. 'Get hold of him!' cried one. He found himself in the arc of a loose

curve of pursuers. He felt suddenly he must be active   5
and resolute.

'You don't understand,' he cried in a voice that was
meant to be great and resolute, and which broke. 'You
are blind, and I can see. Leave me alone!'

'Bogota! Put down that spade, and come off the   10
grass!'

The last order, grotesque in its urban familiarity,
produced a gust of anger.

'I'll hurt you,' he said, sobbing with emotion. 'By
Heaven, I'll hurt you. Leave me alone!'   15

He began to run, not knowing clearly where to run.
He ran from the nearest blind man, because it was a
horror to hit him. He stopped, and then made a dash
to escape from their closing ranks. He made for where a
gap was wide, and the men on either side, with quick   20
perception of the approach of his paces, rushed in on
one another. He sprang forward, and then saw he must
be caught, and *swish!* the spade had struck. He felt the
soft thud of hand and arm, and the man was down with
a yell of pain, and he was through.   25

H. G. WELLS
The Country of the Blind

Vocabulary

groping (l. 1): feeling their way.
blind man's buff (l. 2): a game in which a blindfolded player
    tries to catch others.
grotesque (l. 12): ridiculous, absurd.
swish (l. 23): noise made by the descending spade.
thud (l. 24): dull sound made by the blow.

[2]

He wore a blue serge that nicely fitted his slim figure,
a white shirt with a soft collar, a blue silk tie and brown
shoes. He had had his hair cut short and shaved off the
hair on his face. He looked not only neat, but well-
groomed. It was a transformation. He was very thin;   5

his cheekbones were more prominent, his temples hollower and his eyes in the deep sockets larger than I remembered them; but notwithstanding he looked very well; he looked, indeed, with his deeply sunburnt, unlined face, amazingly young.   10

SOMERSET MAUGHAM

The Razor's Edge

Vocabulary

serge (l. 1): a kind of material; in this sense 'suit'.
transformation (l. 5): change.
temples (l. 6): sides of the head next to the eyes.

[3]

The progress (I do not mean the extension) of education for several centuries has been from one aspect a drift, from another aspect a push; for it has tended to be dominated by the idea of *getting on*. The individual wants more education, not as an aid to the acquisition   5
of wisdom but in order to get on; the nation wants more in order to get the better of other nations, the class wants it to get the better of other classes, or at least to hold its own against them. Education is associated therefore with technical efficiency on the one hand, and with   10
rising in society on the other.

T. S. ELIOT

Modern Education and the Classics

Vocabulary

drift (l. 3): aimless movement.
dominated (l. 4): ruled.
acquisition (l. 5): gaining.
hold its own (ll. 8–9): maintain its position.

You must have noticed that the three passages differ strikingly from each other. The language of the first passage would have been quite out of place if it had been used in the third passage, or vice versa.

The first passage tells a story: the action described is exciting and the reader is carried along quickly by a number of events which occur in rapid succession. A party of blind men surround a sighted man ('Bogota') who is holding a spade. As they close in on him, Bogota springs forward, strikes one of the blind with his spade and breaks through a gap in the ranks. Prose like this which describes an action or a series of actions to tell a story is called *Narrative Prose*.

There is no such sense of movement in the second passage: the prose is static. The writer describes what a man looks like. He begins by giving us details: clothes, hair, cheekbones, eyes, then, as it were, he stands back and comments on the man's general appearance: 'he looked . . . amazingly young'. The man has been described in such a way that it is possible for us to form a definite picture in our minds. This is *Descriptive Prose*, that is, writing which describes scenes, objects, people, or even a person's feelings in such a way that we can imagine them vividly. In good descriptive writing, an author builds up a picture in words in much the same way as an artist paints a landscape or a portrait.

The last passage differs completely from the other two. The writer here is dealing with the problem of education. He argues that education is not sought for its own sake but as a means of 'getting on'. This attitude to education, he writes, affects individuals, society and nations. The result is technical efficiency on the one hand, and a continual effort on the part of people to rise in society by means of education on the other. This sort of prose is *Argumentative*: it is about *ideas*, not about actions or objects. A problem is presented, an argument is built logically round it and often, but not always, the author draws conclusions from his argument, giving his view of the question that he is discussing.

Most prose (though by no means all) falls into one of these three groups: Narrative, Description, Argument. The ability to distinguish between them will help you greatly to understand an author's aims since the *way* an author writes is largely determined by the type of prose he is writing.

You will have noticed how the three writers quoted all use entirely dissimilar methods. This is because they are setting out to do quite different things.

In order to appreciate a prose passage it is not enough to understand its meaning: it is necessary to grasp the author's intentions and the means he has employed to fulfil them. In a sense, good Narrative and Descriptive prose have much in common with poetry. The writer need not always have an audience in mind. His aim is to tell a story or describe a scene as well as he can. The 'devices' that occur arise naturally from the prose itself, and are, as it were, co-incidental with this main purpose. In Argumentative and good journalistic writing, however, the writer *does* have an audience in mind: he may be out to persuade or explain, attack or defend. He is rather in the position of a public speaker who has to keep his audience interested and attentive and he therefore uses devices *consciously* to achieve this purpose. For this reason, Argument differs from other forms of writing and it cannot be appreciated in the same way as Narrative and Description.

6

NARRATIVE
What is it About?

It may seem absurd to say that it is impossible to understand, least of all to appreciate, anything that has been written before you have read it. But in your anxiety to get on with the job of appreciating a piece, it is all too easy to read it in a careless way so that you think you understand it when, in fact, you are only left with a vague impression of what it is about. When reading narrative prose you should observe three important rules:

1. Read the passage carefully so that you really understand it, without worrying over the meaning of a few difficult words.

2. While reading the passage, pay close attention to the sequence of events described or to the stages which lead up to the main event.

3. See if the writer gives reasons why the event or events described occurred.

Try to apply these rules to the following passage.

[1]

June came and the hay was almost ready for cutting. On Midsummer's Eve, which was a Saturday, Mr Jones went into Willingdon and got so drunk at the Red Lion that he did not come back till midday on Sunday. The men had milked the cows in the early morning and then had gone out rabbiting, without bothering to feed the   5

animals. When Mr Jones got back he immediately went
to sleep on the drawing-room sofa with the *News of the
World* over his face, so that when evening came, the
animals were still unfed. At last they could stand it no   10
longer. One of the cows broke in the door of the store-
shed with her horns and all the animals began to help
themselves from the bins. It was just then that Mr Jones
woke up. The next moment he and his four men were in
the store-shed with whips in their hands, lashing out in   15
all directions. This was more than the hungry animals
could bear. With one accord, though nothing of the kind
had been planned beforehand, they flung themselves
upon their tormentors. Jones and his men suddenly
found themselves being butted and kicked from all sides.   20
The situation was quite out of their control. They had
never seen animals behave like this before, and this
sudden uprising of creatures whom they were used to
thrashing and maltreating just as they chose, frightened
them almost out of their wits. After only a moment or   25
two they gave up trying to defend themselves and took
to their heels. A minute later all five of them were in
full flight down the cart-track that led to the main road,
with the animals pursuing them in triumph.

GEORGE ORWELL
Animal Farm

Vocabulary

> lashing out (l. 15): beating wildly with whips.
> with one accord (l. 17): all together.
> tormentors (l. 19): those who were ill-treating them.
> butted (l. 20): pushed (with the head).
> frightened them almost out of their wits (ll. 24–5): i.e., frigh-
> tened them so much that they could no longer act sensibly.

How much of the following did you notice when reading
the passage?

The main event described is the way some animals rise up

against their masters and drive them out of a farm. The sequence of events is as follows:

(i) A cow breaks a door down and all the animals feed from the bins.

(ii) Mr Jones and his men start beating the animals.

(iii) The animals defend themselves against their attackers.

(iv) The men run away and the animals pursue them.

The event described occurred because:

(i) Mr Jones and his men neglected their duties. (Mr Jones had got drunk the night before and did not return to the farm until the next day. The men went rabbiting after milking the cows.)

(ii) Because of this neglect, the animals were hungry.

(iii) The animals were beaten. (It is pointed out, too, that they had often been thrashed on previous occasions.)

FINDING THE MEANING

When you have read a narrative-prose passage carefully, you should be in a position to write down what you think it means. As in poetry, you should give a general meaning, a detailed meaning, and be able to define the intentions of the writer.

General Meaning. This should be based on a reading of the *whole* passage. You should outline the *main event* described in a single sentence.

Detailed Meaning. You should not write a précis of the passage. On the other hand, your account must be accurate and you must not omit essential information. The best way to tackle the detailed meaning is to divide the passage up into what you consider to be its main stages, and then to give a brief account of each stage in a single paragraph. What you have in effect to do is to recount the *essential parts* of the story in your own words.

Intention. A great deal of narrative often does much more than just 'tell a story'. Sometimes there is a deeper meaning behind the story. A writer may relate an event not for the sake of the event alone, but to comment on human behaviour or on society. Frequently this intention behind a narrative piece is implied rather than directly stated. This does not mean to say that *all* narrative conceals a deeper meaning: a writer very often sets out to do nothing more than to tell a story well. Never read into a piece intentions which have neither been implied nor expressed.

Read the passage below and give its general and detailed meaning. When you have done so, write what you consider to be the author's intention. Then compare what you have written with the passage that follows.

[2]

The old man dropped the line and put his foot on it and lifted the harpoon as high as he could and drove it down with all his strength, and more strength he had just summoned, into the fish's side just behind the great chest fin that rose high in the air to the altitude of the 5 man's chest. He felt the iron go in and he leaned on it and drove it further and then pushed all his weight after it.

Then the fish came alive, with his death in him, and rose high out of the water showing all his great length 10 and width and all his power and his beauty. He seemed to hang in the air above the old man in the skiff. Then he fell into the water with a crash that sent spray over the old man and over all of the skiff.

The old man felt faint and sick and he could not see 15 well. But he cleared the harpoon line and let it run slowly through his raw hands and, when he could see, he saw the fish was on his back with his silver belly up. The shaft of the harpoon was projecting at an angle from the fish's shoulder and the sea was discolouring 20 with the red of the blood from his heart. First it was dark as a shoal in the blue water that was more than a mile deep. Then it spread like a cloud. The fish was silvery and still and floated with the waves.

The old man looked carefully in the glimpse of vision 25 that he had. Then he took two turns of the harpoon line around the bitt in the bow and laid his head on his hands.

'Keep my head clear,' he said against the wood of the bow. 'I am a tired old man. But I have killed this fish 30 which is my brother and now I must do the slave work.'

ERNEST HEMINGWAY

The Old Man and the Sea

Vocabulary

skiff (l. 14): light rowing boat.

bitt (l. 27): one of two posts called *bitts*, used for fastening cables.

General meaning, detailed meaning and intention. Ernest Hemingway describes how an old man killed an enormous fish.

As the great fish rose into the air, the old man, summoning all his strength, drove his harpoon into its side. This made the fish leap right out of the water and then crash down heavily covering the man and his boat with spray. The old man felt dazed, but he let out the harpoon line. When he recovered, he saw his harpoon had pierced the fish's shoulder. The great fish lay motionless on its back and its dark blood discoloured the blue water. After looking at it for a while, the old man laid his head in his hands and thought of the fish he had killed.

This is the story of a struggle which brings out a man's finest qualities. The man speaks of himself as being a 'tired old man', yet, at a critical moment, he has been able to summon all his strength and ingenuity to kill a creature which is many times bigger and more powerful than he is. The old man does not gloat over his victory. If anything, he is sad: he regards the fish as his equal and refers to it as his 'brother'.

EXERCISES ON FINDING THE MEANING

Answer the questions on the three passages that follow, bearing in mind the example you have just read.

[3]

The following evening was very wet: indeed it poured down till day-dawn; and, as I took my morning walk round the house, I observed the master's window swinging open, and the rain driving straight in. He cannot be in bed, I thought: those showers would drench him 5 through. He must either be up or out. But I'll make no more ado, I'll go boldly and look.

Having succeeded in obtaining entrance with another key, I ran to unclose the panels, for the chamber was vacant; quickly pushing them aside, I peeped in. Mr 10 Heathcliff was there—laid on his back. His eyes met mine so keen and fierce, I started; and then he seemed to smile. I could not think him dead; but his face and throat were washed with rain; the bedclothes dripped, and he was perfectly still. The lattice, flapping to and 15 fro, had grazed one hand that rested on the sill; no blood trickled from the broken skin, and when I put my fingers to it, I could doubt no more: he was dead and stark!

I hasped the window; I combed his long black hair from his forehead; I tried to close his eyes; to extinguish, 20 if possible, that frightful, life-like gaze of exultation before any one else beheld it. They would not shut: they seemed to sneer at my attempts: and his parted lips and sharp white teeth sneered too!

EMILY BRONTË
Wuthering Heights

Vocabulary

I'll make no more ado (ll. 6–7): I'll not make any more fuss about it.

lattice (l. 15): a window opening on side hinges and having small panes of glass held in position by narrow strips of lead.

flapping (l. 15): swinging.

grazed (l. 16): scratched slightly.

stark (l. 18): rigid, stiff.

hasped (l. 19): fastened.

QUESTIONS

1. What attracted the narrator's attention to the bedroom?
2. How did the narrator gain entrance to the room?
3. 'I could not think him dead' (l. 13). Why not?
4. What expression did the dead man have on his face?
5. Write the general and detailed meaning of the passage and what you consider to be the writer's intention.

[4]

O'Malley was the frightening master at Boystone School. There was always silence when he came scraping one sarcastic foot into the room, showing his small teeth with the grin of one about to feast off human vanity.

He was a man of fifty with a head like an otter's on 5 which the hair was drying and dying. He had a dry, hay-like moustache, flattened Irish nostrils. He walked with small pedantic, waltzing steps, as though he had a hook pulling at the seat of his trousers and was being dandled along by a chain. Mr O'Malley was a terrorist. He turned 10 to face the boys, by his silence daring them to move, speak or even breathe. When he had silenced them, he walked two more steps, and then turned suddenly to stare again. He was twisting the screw of silence tighter and tighter. After two minutes had passed and the 15 silence was absolute, he gave a small sharp sniff of contempt, and put his hands under the remains of his rotting rusty gown and walked to his desk.

V. S. PRITCHETT

Mr Beluncle

Vocabulary

dandled (l. 9): being danced along as if he were a marionette.

terrorist (l. 10): one who kept control by inspiring terror in his pupils.

gown (l. 18): long, loose-fitting garment, usually black in colour, worn by teachers, judges, members of a university, etc.

1. What information does the writer give us about: (a) O'Malley's appearance, (b) his character, (c) his attitude to the boys at Boystone School?

2. Write the general and detailed meaning of the passage and what you consider to be the writer's intention.

[5]

I was startled when the bill of fare was brought, for the prices were a great deal higher than I had anticipated. But she reassured me.

'I never eat anything for luncheon,' she said.

'Oh, don't say that!' I answered generously.   5

'I never eat more than one thing. I think people eat far too much nowadays. A little fish, perhaps. I wonder if they have any salmon.'

Well, it was early in the year for salmon and it was not on the bill of fare, but I asked the waiter if there was any. 10 Yes, a beautiful salmon had just come in, it was the first they had had. I ordered it for my guest. The waiter asked her if she would have something while it was being cooked.

'No,' she answered, 'I never eat more than one thing. 15 Unless you had a little caviare. I never mind caviare.'

My heart sank a little. I knew I could not afford caviare, but I could not very well tell her that. I told the waiter by all means to bring caviare. For myself I chose the cheapest dish on the menu and that was a 20 mutton chop.

'I think you're unwise to eat meat,' she said. 'I don't know how you can expect to work after eating heavy things like chops. I don't believe in overloading my stomach.' 25

Then came the question of drink.

'I never drink anything for luncheon,' she said.

'Neither do I,' I answered promptly.

'Except white wine,' she proceeded as though I had

not spoken. 'These French white wines are so light. 30
They're wonderful for the digestion.'

'What would you like?' I asked, hospitable still, but
not exactly effusive.

She gave me a bright and amicable flash of her white
teeth.   35

'My doctor won't let me drink anything but cham-
pagne.'

SOMERSET MAUGHAM
The Luncheon

Vocabulary

anticipated (ll. 2–3): expected.
effusive (l. 33): hearty, encouraging.
amicable (l. 34): friendly.

QUESTIONS

1. Why was the writer in a difficult position?
2. How does the writer imply that his guest was an insensitive
   sort of person?
3. 'Oh, don't say that!' I answered *generously*. (l. 5). 'What would
   you like?' I asked, hospitable still, *but not exactly effusive*.
   (ll. 32–33). Give reasons for the writer's changed attitude to his
   guest.
4. Write the general and detailed meaning of the passage and
   what you consider to be the writer's intention.

How it is Done

APPRECIATING NARRATIVE PROSE

You may have noticed how difficult it is sometimes to say
why you have enjoyed or disliked a particular book or film.
Appreciation of prose amounts to just this: the ability to
state why you have enjoyed what you have read. But to do
this you have to understand *how* a story has been written.

The first thing to realize is that a story, when reduced to

its barest essentials, is usually unexciting. The main events of a long and interesting novel could be retold in a few words, but they would, of course, be flat and dull. What makes a story a pleasure to read is the writer's way of telling it. The way scenes and people are described, for instance, and the way the characters think, talk or act are quite as important as the events themselves and contribute largely to our enjoyment. When appreciating narrative prose, it is necessary to show how these qualities or *devices* help a story to develop and how they add colour to it. Since they are a natural part of a good story, we can only find them when we analyse what we are reading.

In the following explanation of devices, all the examples have been drawn from the passages you have already studied.

STRUCTURAL DEVICES

Unity, Contrast, Description, Dialogue.

Unity. Although none of the narrative passages in this book is complete in itself in the sense that a poem is complete, they all, nevertheless, deal with a main event. When considering unity, you should show how a piece of narrative prose has been put together, but you must take very great care not to repeat your account of the detailed meaning. You should observe how everything that happens in the story contributes to the main event, pointing out anything you consider to be irrelevant.

Notice in the passage from *Animal Farm* by George Orwell, how the main event, the rising of the animals against their masters, is the direct result of all that has gone before: Mr Jones' drunkenness, the men's negligence and subsequent cruelty, and the hunger of the animals. The men take to their heels because 'they had never seen animals behave in this way before'. Though the outcome is rather surprising, the author has prepared the reader for it by giving him details which lead to it.

Similarly, in the passage from *The Old Man and the Sea*, the events follow in logical succession. The climax here is reached in the second paragraph where the fish leaps into the air and crashes down beside the skiff. The old man only realizes that the fish is dead when he sees the harpoon sticking in its side. This leads him to think about the fish.

Emile Brontë in *Wuthering Heights* arouses our curiosity with a small detail: 'the master's window swinging open'. Here, although we are led up to a climax, we are not prepared for it: the writer sets out to take us by surprise. The narrator, seeing the window open, concludes that the master 'must either be up or out' only to find that he is dead. Notice how a simple and seemingly unimportant detail leads the narrator to make this startling discovery.

The repetition of a single phrase gives the passage from *The Luncheon* its unity. When we first come across the sentence, 'I never eat more than one thing', we take it at its face value. But the 'one thing' turns into salmon and caviare, so when the guest says, 'I never drink anything for luncheon', we can suspect that she will (and as it turns out, she does) order something expensive.

Contrast, the placing of opposite pictures side by side, is very often used to balance a narrative and keep the reader simultaneously interested in two things at once. Two situations run parallel until they finally meet; the point at which they meet is often a climax in the story.

Contrast occurs in the passages from *Animal Farm*, from *The Old Man and the Sea*, and from *The Luncheon*. In the first, there are two situations: the men are lazy; the animals unfed. This leads to a climax where the positions are reversed: the animals become 'masters'. There are similarly two opposites in the second passage: there is 'the tired old man' on the one hand and the fish with 'his great length and width and all his power and beauty' on the other. The fish's appearance symbolizes the noble spirit of the old man who summons enough strength to kill it, yet still considers it his brother. In the last piece, a rather complicated game is being played between the host and his guest. This delicate balance is sustained all the way through as the host's position gets steadily worse and worse.

Description. It is virtually impossible to have narrative without description for it is by this means that an author sets his scene and gives his reader a sense of time and place. At the same time, in good narrative there is never description *for its own sake.* It always adds something to the story and directly or indirectly influences the course of events.

In *The Old Man and the Sea*, the description of the dead fish with its blood discolouring the water, enables the old man to see how great and splendid is the creature he has killed and leads him to think about it.

We have already seen how the description of the swinging window leads to the discovery of a dead man in *Wuthering Heights*. There is something horrific in the description of the dead man that follows: his eyes will not shut; they have a 'frightful, life-like gaze' and seem to sneer—as do his 'parted lips and sharp white teeth'. The whole passage relies heavily on description for the atmosphere of mystery and horror which is created.

The sentence 'Mr O'Malley was a terrorist' in the passage from *Mr Beluncle* would be quite meaningless if it were not accompanied by a detailed description of O'Malley's appearance and behaviour. Only when we have understood what sort of person he is can we understand the absolute silence he commands in class.

Dialogue. A writer helps his characters to come alive not only by describing the way they act but by letting us hear them speak. Effective dialogue enables the reader to feel that he is actually witnessing what is going on.

The passage from *The Luncheon* is built almost entirely of dialogue. The guest's tone does not alter throughout as she goes on deceiving herself and her host into believing that she eats very little and then promptly ordering the most expensive items on the menu. At the beginning the host is obviously anxious to please his guest, but his tone becomes more and more subdued as time passes: he is somewhat less 'generous' at the end, than he was at the beginning.

When considering dialogue, always observe how a writer

makes the *tone* vary in the words spoken by different characters.

SENSE DEVICES

Style, Use of words, Metaphor, Simile.

Style. When we speak of a writer's 'style' we mean the way
he handles all devices generally. Style is the quality that
makes one piece of writing different from another and is
thus one of the most important characteristics of prose. A
writer must take very great care to adapt his style of writing
to his subject-matter.

You will have noticed how strikingly different in style are
all the pieces you have studied. The extract from *Animal
Farm* is simple and direct: it is written in a matter-of-fact
way. The pace of the story is fast. The same is true of the
passage from *Wuthering Heights*. The story develops rapidly:
at one moment we are looking up at a window; at the next,
at a dead man. The reader is taken by surprise in both
passages precisely because of the deceptively simple style.
The passage from *The Old Man and the Sea* has the quality
of simplicity, but it is far from being matter-of-fact. If you
read the passage aloud you may discover that the style has
a rhythm which is nearer poetry than prose. And by comparison with the other two pieces, the pace of the narrative
is slow: the reader lingers over details: exactly how the old
man threw the harpoon; the fish's blood colouring the
water, etc. The style of *Mr Beluncle*, by comparison, is
complex. The pace is very slow indeed, as the reader is
obliged to stop after each sentence to grasp all its implica-
tions: O'Malley's hair is 'drying and dying', he walks 'as
though he had a hook pulling at the seat of his trousers'.
The style in fact mimics O'Malley's character: like him it is
pedantic and over-meticulous.

Use of Words, Metaphor, Simile. The way an author handles
words not only gives his style of writing a definite quality
but adds colour to his narrative and enables the reader to
imagine more readily what is happening.

Hemingway relies largely on simple words in *The Old Man and the Sea*. The apparent contradiction of the sentence 'Then the fish came alive, with his death in him' prepares us for the great leap the fish makes out of the water. The comparison of the fish's blood to a whole 'shoal' of fish and then to a 'cloud' billowing darkly under the blue water, very vividly stresses the fish's great size and majesty.

Notice how much the words 'sarcastic', 'haylike', 'pedantic', 'waltzing', 'rotting', and 'rusty' tell us about O'Malley's character in *Mr Beluncle*, even though they are used here to describe his manner and appearance. The metaphors 'to feast off human vanity' and 'twisting the screw of silence' similarly indicate vividly how much the teacher enjoys making his helpless victims suffer.

In *Wuthering Heights*, the repeated word 'sneer' adds to the horror of the description of the dead man. Heathcliff's expression is devoid of all calm: he has a 'frightful life-like gaze'; in a sense he continues to live, even though he is dead.

Comment briefly on the use of words in *The Luncheon* and *Animal Farm*. What phrases seem to you especially vivid and what do they contribute to the narrative?

EXERCISES ON APPRECIATION

[1]

Suddenly he heard a shriek, and he flung the spade from him and started for the bridge, looking up like a startled deer. Ah, there was Winifred—Joyce had hurt herself. He went on up the garden.

'What is it?'   5

The child was still screaming—now it was—'Daddy! Daddy! Oh-oh, Daddy!' And the mother was saying:

'Don't be frightened, darling. Let mother look.'

But the child only cried:

'Oh, Daddy, Daddy, Daddy!'   10

She was terrified by the sight of the blood running from her own knee. Winifred crouched down, with her

D

child of six in her lap, to examine the knee. Egbert bent over also.

'Don't make such a noise, Joyce,' he said irritably. 15 'How did she do it?'

'She fell on that sickle thing which you left lying about after cutting the grass,' said Winifred, looking into his face with bitter accusation as he bent near.

He had taken his handkerchief and tied it round the 20 knee. Then he lifted the still sobbing child in his arms, and carried her into the house and upstairs to her bed. In his arms she became quiet. But his heart was burning with pain and with guilt.

D. H. LAWRENCE

England My England

Vocabulary

> sickle (l. 17): curved blade fitted into a short wooden handle, used for cutting grass.
>
> thing (l. 17): i.e., she is not quite sure that she is using the correct term.

QUESTIONS

1. Give the general and detailed meaning of the passage and what you consider to be the writer's intention.

2. In what different ways are the husband (Egbert) and the wife (Winifred) affected by their child's accident? How is this brought out in the dialogue?

3. Comment on the *tone* of words spoken by the child, the mother and the father.

4. Comment on the writer's style. Is the pace of the narrative fast or slow? Give reasons for your answer.

[2]

Without another word she dressed quickly, almost viciously. From the road outside the low rumble of passing vehicles reached her, with the sharp clap of horses' feet and an occasional shout. When she had finished her hasty dressing she drew up the blind in   5

impatient jerks and looked down into the street below.
Between the long gulf of dark houses was passing a
ragged procession of wagonettes, carts, vans and traps,
each with its pair of lamps shining over the shadowy
figures of the rider, men and women and even children,   10
huddled together in the chill summer darkness. The
sight seemed to weary her afresh and suddenly she blew
out the candle fiercely. In the other houses there were
no lights, and except for the lamps passing endlessly
below, and a few stars hanging over the roofs in the clear   15
sky, the sombre darkness was unbroken.

As she was descending the stairs, the warm smell of
fresh-baked bread rose and met her. In a moment her
nostrils seemed to quiver with nausea and she stood
still, trembling. Then her husband came running from   20
the bake-house, loaded with a great basket of fancy rolls.
She could hear his breath hissing through his teeth. He
caught sight of her standing there, and shouted as he
passed out: 'Don't stand there like a dummy! Do something! You see how late we are!'   25

H. E. BATES
The Baker's Wife

Vocabulary

traps (l. 8): carriages.

quiver with nausea (l. 19): to tremble as if she was going to be
sick.

dummy (l. 24): in this sense, a helpless fool, a useless object.

QUESTIONS

1. Give the general and detailed meaning of the passage and what
you consider to be the writer's intention.

2. Comment briefly on the unity of the passage.

3. How does the description given in the first paragraph affect
the pace of the narrative?

4. How does the writer imply that the husband and wife are not
on good terms? Comment on his choice of words.

[3]

Ralph wormed his way through the thicket towards the forest, keeping as far as possible beneath the smoke. Presently he saw open space, and the green leaves of the edge of the thicket. A smallish savage was standing between him and the rest of the forest, a savage striped red 5 and white, and carrying a spear. He was coughing and smearing the paint about his eyes with the back of his hand as he tried to see through the increasing smoke. Ralph launched himself like a cat; stabbed, snarling, with the spear, and the savage doubled up. There was 10 a shout from beyond the thicket and then Ralph was running with the swiftness of fear through the undergrowth. He came to a pig-run, followed it for perhaps a hundred yards, and then swerved off. Behind him the ululation swept across the island once more and a single 15 voice shouted three times. He guessed that was the signal to advance and sped away again till his chest was like fire. Then he flung himself down under a bush and waited for a moment till his breathing steadied. He passed his tongue tentatively over his teeth and lips and 20 heard far off the ululation of the pursuers.

WILLIAM GOLDING

Lord of the Flies

Vocabulary

wormed his way (l. 1): made his way by crawling.
thicket (l. 1): trees growing close together.
launched himself (l. 9): sprang forward.
undergrowth (ll. 12–13): small shrubs and trees.
ululation (l. 15): howling, prolonged shouting.
tentatively (l. 20): uncertainly, as if unsure of himself.

QUESTIONS

1. Give the general and detailed meaning of the passage and what you consider to be the writer's intention.

2. How does the writer convey Ralph's fear?

3. Comment on the writer's attention to detail.
4. In what way does the pace of the narrative suit the subject-matter?

Literary Appreciation

When writing full literary appreciation in continuous prose, it is not enough to point out the devices: you must say how they affect the course of the narrative. The passages that follow will not, of course, contain *all* the devices you have studied. In each case, the devices will vary with the nature of the narrative.

The key given below should serve as a guide. It reminds you of what you have to do when appreciating narrative prose and indicates how you should lay out your paragraphs.

KEY

I. READING	Read carefully, observing what happens and why it happens.
2. MEANING	*General*
	Detailed: the main stages of the story.
	Intention: implied or stated.
3. DEVICES	
(a) STRUCTURAL	*Unity*: do *not* repeat the detailed meaning.
	Contrast
	Description
	Dialogue
(b) SENSE	*Style*
	Use of Words, metaphor, simile.

Before going on to the passages that follow, study the appreciation of the extract from *The Old Man and the Sea.* Your own work should be roughly along these lines.

Ernest Hemingway describes how an old man killed an enormous fish.

As the great fish rose into the air, the old man, summoning

all his strength, drove his harpoon into its side. This made
the fish leap right out of the water and then crash down
heavily covering the man and his boat with spray. The old
man felt dazed, but he let out the harpoon line. When he
recovered, he saw his harpoon had pierced the fish's shoulder. The great fish lay motionless on its back and its dark
blood discoloured the blue water. After looking at it for a
while, the old man laid his head in his hands and thought of
the fish he had killed.

This is the story of a struggle which brings out a man's
finest qualities. The man speaks of himself as being a
'tired old man', yet, at a critical moment, he has been able
to summon all his strength and ingenuity to kill a creature
which is many times bigger and more powerful than he is.
The old man does not gloat over his victory. If anything,
he is sad: he regards the fish as his equal and refers to it as
his 'brother'.

The narrative falls into two distinct parts: action and its
consequences. What the man sees and feels after he kills
the fish is not less important than the description of the
killing and follows logically from it.

Hemingway is dealing with two completely different
things: a man and a fish. At the beginning of the passage
they are enemies; at the end they are 'brothers'. In this
passage there is no description for its own sake: whatever is
said about the man and the fish has a direct bearing on the
narrative, and points to the contrast between the two. The
man is old and tired; the fish huge and powerful. Both of
them summon their last reserves of strength in the struggle
and victory falls to the man. The description of the huge
fish lying dead on the water is absolutely necessary to the
story: it is what the old man sees that makes him feel sym-
pathy for the creature he has killed.

The style throughout is extremely simple; the description of the action detailed and exact. At the same time it is
never commonplace or tedious: the prose has a distinct
rhythm of its own. Nothing is hurried. The events occur in
slow motion so that the reader can follow each stage of the

narrative in detail. A good example of this occurs in the lines: 'Then the fish came alive, with his death in him, and rose high out of the water showing all his great length and width, and all his power and his beauty.' The repeated word 'and' isolates each of the fish's qualities so that it appears truly magnificent. The dead fish is vividly described later through the writer's references to colour and the brilliant comparisons he draws: the sea is blue, the fish silver, while beneath it, its dark blood spreads like a 'shoal' and then 'like a cloud'. It is these details which stress the calm that follows the battle and arouse feelings of awe and kinship in the old man for the fish he has killed.

Write an appreciation of each of the passages that follow.

[1]

I was standing at the end of the lower play-ground and annoying Mr Samuels, who lived in the house just below the high railings. Mr Samuels complained once a week that boys from the school threw apples and stones and balls through his bedroom window. He sat in a 5 deck chair in a small square of trim garden and tried to read the newspaper. I was only a few yards from him. I was staring him out. He pretended not to notice me, but I knew he knew I was standing there rudely and quietly. Every now and then he peeped at me from be- 10 hind his newspaper, saw me still and serious and alone, with my eyes on his. As soon as he lost his temper I was going to go home. Already I was late for dinner. I had almost beaten him, the newspaper was trembling, he was breathing heavily, when a strange boy, whom I had 15 not heard approach, pushed me down the bank.

I threw a stone at his face. He took off his spectacles, put them in his coat pocket, took off his coat, hung it neatly on the railings, and attacked. Turning round as we wrestled on the top of the bank, I saw that Mr 20 Samuels had folded his newspaper on the deck chair and was standing up to watch us. It was a mistake to turn

round. The strange boy rabbit-punched me twice. Mr
Samuels hopped with excitement as I fell against the
railings. I was down in the dust, hot and scratched and   25
biting, then up and dancing, and I butted the boy in the
belly and we tumbled in a heap. I saw through a closing
eye that his nose was bleeding. I hit his nose. He tore
at my collar and spun me round by the hair.

'Come on! come on!' I heard Mr Samuels cry.   30

We both turned towards him. He was shaking his fists
and dodging about in the garden. He stopped then, and
coughed, and set his panama straight, and avoided our
eyes, and turned his back and walked slowly to the deck
chair.   35

We both threw gravel at him.

DYLAN THOMAS

Portrait of the Artist as a Young Dog

Vocabulary

> trim (l. 6): neat.
> I was staring him out (ll. 7–8): I was gazing fixedly into his
> eyes so as to cause him to turn away.
> rabbit-punched me (l. 23): he hit me in the back of the neck.
> I butted (l. 26): I hit him with my head.
> panama (l. 33): hat of flexible, closely woven straw.
> gravel (l. 36): small stones used for laying paths.

[2]

After a while, . . . we could hear one voice calling
'Murder!' and another voice, 'Convicts! Runaways!
Guard! This way for the runaway convicts!' Then both
voices would seem to be stifled in a struggle, and then
would break out again. And when it had come to this,   5
the soldiers ran like deer, and Joe too.

The sergeant ran in first, when we had run the noise
quite down, and two of his men ran in close upon him.
Their pieces were cocked and levelled when we all ran
in.

'Here are both men!' panted the sergeant, struggling   10

at the bottom of a ditch. 'Surrender, you two! and confound you for two wild beasts! Come asunder!'

Water was splashing, and mud was flying, and oaths were being sworn, and blows were being struck, when some more men went down into the ditch to help the 15 sergeant, and dragged out, separately, my convict and the other one. Both were bleeding and panting and execrating and struggling; but of course I knew them both directly.

'Mind!' said my convict, wiping blood from his face 20 with his ragged sleeves, and shaking torn hair from his fingers; '*I* took him! *I* give him up to you! Mind that!'

'It's not much to be particular about,' said the sergeant; 'it'll do you small good, my man, being in the same plight yourself. Handcuffs there!' 25

'I don't expect it to do me any good. I don't want it to do me more good than it does me now,' said my convict, with a greedy laugh. 'I took him. He knows it. That's enough for me.'

The other convict was livid to look at, and, in addition 30 to the old bruised left side of his face, seemed to be bruised and torn all over. He could not so much as get his breath to speak, until they were both separately handcuffed, but leaned upon a soldier to keep himself from falling. 35

'Take notice, guard—he tried to murder me,' were his first words.

'Tried to murder him?' said my convict disdainfully. 'Try, and not do it?'

CHARLES DICKENS

Great Expectations

Vocabulary

we had run the noise quite down (ll. 7–8): we had discovered, exactly, the place where the noise was coming from.

their pieces were cocked and levelled (l. 9): their guns were made ready for firing and aimed at the men.

asunder (l. 12): apart.

execrating (l. 18): cursing.
livid (l. 30): bluish-coloured (because of his bruises).

[3]

When I was very young—I could not have been more
than five years old—we were living in the country not
so far from a large garrison town, although we seldom
saw any soldiers, and we had heard from an uncle who
was in the Cavalry that his regiment would be riding   5
past on their way to the summer manœuvres, so this
morning my mother had taken me down to the main
road to see them go by.

It was a lovely summer morning, I remember, and we
were standing in a meadow overlooking the road. As   10
soon as I heard the horses' hooves in the distance coming
at a trot along the hard road, I was seized with a feeling
of most frightening panic and frantic desire to hide or
run away. I remember holding my mother's hand very
tightly and the feeling of panic not really subsiding until   15
all the soldiers had gone past and the sound of the
horses' hooves had died away in the distance. I have
often wondered if there are other people who feel like
this, or if it is explained by a recurring dream I had in
my childhood. I cannot now remember if the first time   20
I had this dream was before or after the occasion of the
soldiers, but I dreamt this same dream several times in
my childhood.

I was awakened from my sleep—it seemed to be very late
in the night, in a room in which I had not gone to sleep,   25
and in quite a different bed, by a pleasant woman who
seemed to be my nurse, and who, with low soothing
noises, dressed me in clothes which again were not the
clothes I had taken off. I was put into a little suit, I
remember, of some dark cloth with rather baggy knick-   30
ers, and a pair of stout leather shoes. The woman too
was wearing a dark cloth dress and a long, dark cloak
with a hood. I was dressed very quickly and then we
went down a wide uncarpeted staircase into a large oak-

beamed room in which there were a number of people. 35
The room was dimly lit and there was not much furniture, but what there was was very massive.

As we came into the room a man and a woman detached themselves from a group and came towards us.
The man was tall and splendid and the woman I thought 40
very pretty. She knelt down and took me into her arms,
and I saw that she was crying. She hugged me to her,
kissing me again and again, until the man gently took
me away and the nurse again took my hand. The big
door was unbarred and opened just wide enough for us 45
to slip through. Outside it was a bright moonlit night
and an empty street. The nurse and I went to the left up
this street, keeping very close to the wall. Suddenly
there was the sound of horses' hooves ringing on the
cobbled street and the woman quickly pulled me behind 50
a buttress and drew me under her cloak. We crouched
there in the dark corner while a troop of horsemen rode
by, and on each man's left arm was tied a white handkerchief. After they had gone by, we waited a little, then
the woman took me by the hand and ran with me across 55
the street into an alleyway which seemed to slope down
to a river, but whether it was a river or not I never knew
for the dream always ended there.

TOM HARRISON

Ghosts and Dreams

Vocabulary

garrison town (l. 3): town in which troops are stationed.
cavalry (l. 5): regiment of horse soldiers.
manœuvres (l. 6): military exercises.
at a trot (l. 12): at a moderate pace.
frantic (l. 13): wild, uncontrollable.
subsiding (l. 15): abating, becoming calm.
recurring dream (l. 19): one that occurs again and again.
baggy knickers (ll. 30–1): loose-fitting trousers reaching from
    waist to knees, where they are fastened with a band.
stout (l. 31): sturdy, strong.

detached themselves (ll. 38–9): came away from.
cobbled (l. 50): paved with round stones.
buttress (l. 51): support built against a wall.
alleyway (l. 56): narrow street.

[4]

The chief magistrate was a venerable-looking man, with white hair and beard and a face of great sagacity. He looked me all over for about five minutes, letting his eyes wander from the crown of my head to the soles of my feet, up and down, and down and up; neither did his mind seem in the least clearer when he had done looking than when he began. He at length asked me a single short question, which I supposed meant 'Who are you?' I answered in English quite composedly as though he would understand me, and endeavoured to be my very most natural self as well as I could. He appeared more and more puzzled, and then retired, returning with two others much like himself. Then they took me into an inner room, and the two fresh arrivals stripped me, while the chief looked on. They felt my pulse, they looked at my tongue, they listened at my chest, they felt all my muscles; and at the end of each operation they looked at the chief and nodded, and said something in a tone quite pleasant, as though I were all right. They even pulled down my eyelids, and looked, I suppose, to see if they were bloodshot; but it was not so. At length they gave up; and I think that all were satisfied of my being in the most perfect health, and very robust to boot. At last the old magistrate made me a speech of about five minutes long, which the other two appeared to think greatly to the point, but from which I gathered nothing. As soon as it was ended, they proceeded to overhaul my swag and the contents of my pockets. This gave me little uneasiness, for I had no money with me, nor anything which they were at all likely to want, or which I cared about losing. At least I fancied so, but I soon found my mistake.

They got on comfortably at first, though they were
much puzzled with my tobacco-pipe and insisted on
seeing me use it. When I had shown them what I did 35
with it, they were astonished but not displeased, and
seemed to like the smell. But by and by they came to my
watch, which I had hidden away in the inmost pocket
that I had, and had forgotten when they began their
search. They seemed concerned and uneasy as soon as 40
they got hold of it. They then made me open it and show
the works; and when I had done so they gave signs of
very grave displeasure which disturbed me all the more
because I could not conceive wherein it could have
offended them.   45

SAMUEL BUTLER

Erewhon

Vocabulary

venerable-looking man (l. 1): a man who looked worthy of
   deep respect.
sagacity (l. 2): wisdom.
done (l. 6): finished.
composedly (l. 9): calmly.
robust to boot (l. 23): strong as well.
to overhaul my swag (ll.27–8): to examine my belongings.

[5]

The door opened quietly and closed. A quick whisper
ran through the class: the prefect of studies. There was
an instant of dead silence and then the loud crack of a
pandybat on the last desk. Stephen's heart leapt up in
fear.   5
—Any boys want flogging here, Father Arnall? cried
the prefect of studies. Any lazy idle loafers that want
flogging in this class?
He came to the middle of the class and saw Fleming
on his knees.   10
—Hoho! he cried. Who is this boy? Why is he on his
knees? What is your name, boy?

—Fleming, sir.

—Hoho, Fleming! An idler of course. I can see it in
your eye. Why is he on his knees, Father Arnall?   15

—He wrote a bad Latin theme, Father Arnall said,
and he missed all the questions in grammar.

—Of course he did! cried the prefect of studies, of
course he did! A born idler! I can see it in the corner of
his eye.   20

He banged his pandybat down on the desk and cried:

—Up, Fleming! Up, my boy!

Fleming stood up slowly.

—Hold out! cried the prefect of studies.

Fleming held out his hand. The pandybat came down 25
on it with a loud smacking sound: one, two, three, four,
five, six.

—Other hand!

The pandybat came down again in six loud quick
smacks.   30

—Kneel down! cried the prefect of studies.

Fleming knelt down squeezing his hands under his
armpits, his face contorted with pain, but Stephen knew
how hard his hands were because Fleming was always
rubbing rosin into them. But perhaps he was in great 35
pain for the noise of the pandybat was terrible. Stephen's
heart was beating and fluttering.

—At your work, all of you! shouted the prefect of
studies. We want no lazy idle loafers here, lazy idle
little schemers. At your work, I tell you. Father Dolan 40
will be in to see you every day. Father Dolan will be in
tomorrow.

He poked one of the boys in the side with the pandybat, saying:

—You, boy! When will Father Dolan be in again?   45

—Tomorrow, sir, said Tom Furlong's voice.

—Tomorrow and tomorrow and tomorrow, said the
prefect of studies. Make up your minds for that. Every
day Father Dolan. Write away. You, boy, who are you?

Stephen's heart jumped suddenly.   50

—Dedalus, sir.

—Why are you not writing like the others?

—I . . . my . . .

He could not speak with fright.

—Why is he not writing, Father Arnall?   55

—He broke his glasses, said Father Arnall, and I exempted him from work.

—Broke? What is this I hear? What is this? Your name is? said the prefect of studies.

—Dedalus, sir.   60

—Out here, Dedalus. Lazy little schemer. I see schemer in your face.

JAMES JOYCE

Portrait of the Artist as a Young Man

Vocabulary

pandybat (l. 4): cane, stick used for the express purpose of beating.

flogging (l. 6): beating.

loafers (l. 7): lazy people.

contorted (l. 33): twisted.

rosin (l. 35): i.e., a resin, sticky substance produced by plants.

schemers (l. 40): in this sense, boys who make secret plans to avoid work.

Father Dolan (l. 40): i.e., the prefect of studies.

[6]

The two horses came up close to me, looking with great earnestness upon my face and hands. The gray steed rubbed my hat all round with his right fore-hoof, and discomposed it so much that I was forced to adjust it better, by taking it off, and settling it again; whereat   5
both he and his companion (who was a brown bay) appeared to be much surprised; the latter felt the lappet of my coat, and finding it to hang loose about me, they both looked with new signs of wonder. He stroked my right hand, seeming to admire the softness and colour;   10
but he squeezed it so hard between his hoof and his

pastern, that I was forced to roar; after which they both touched me with all possible tenderness. They were under great perplexity about my shoes and stockings, which they felt very often, neighing to each other, and using various gestures, not unlike those of a philosopher, when he would attempt to solve some new and difficult phenomenon.

Upon the whole, the behaviour of these animals was so orderly and rational, so acute and judicious, that I at last concluded they must needs be magicians, who had thus metamorphosed themselves upon some design, and seeing a stranger in the way, were resolved to divert themselves with him; or perhaps were really amazed at the sight of a man so very different in habit, feature, and complexion from those who might probably live in so remote a climate. Upon the strength of this reasoning, I ventured to address them in the following manner: Gentlemen, if you be conjurers, as I have good cause to believe, you can understand my language; therefore I make so bold to let your worships know that I am a poor distressed Englishman, driven by his misfortunes upon your coast, and I entreat one of you, to let me ride upon his back, as if he were a real horse, to some house or village where I can be relieved. In return of which favour I will make you a present of this knife and bracelet (taking them out of my pocket). The two creatures stood silent while I spoke, seeming to listen with great attention; and when I had ended, they neighed frequently towards each other, as if they were engaged in serious conversation.

JONATHAN SWIFT
Gulliver's Travels

Vocabulary

steed (l. 3): horse.
discomposed (l. 4): deranged, knocked it out of place.
whereat (l. 5): upon which.
bay (l. 6): reddish-brown horse.

lappet (l. 7): lapel.

pastern (l. 12): part of horse's leg just above the hoof.

they were under great perplexity (ll. 13–14): they were very
puzzled.

judicious (l. 20): sensible.

must needs be (l. 21): i.e., must be.

metamorphosed (l. 22): changed.

divert (l. 23): amuse.

habit (l. 25): dress.

conjurers (l. 29): magicians.

your worships (l. 31): form of address used to show respect
for persons of higher rank.

relieved (l. 35): in this sense, assisted, taken care of.

7

DESCRIPTION
What is it About?

In narrative prose, any descriptive passages that may occur are important only in so far as they contribute to the main purpose of the narrative. Prose that is purely descriptive has no such secondary purpose: it aims at creating a definite atmosphere of its own. Because there is no obvious story attached to descriptive prose, you may very easily be led to read it carelessly. When reading description you should observe these rules:

1. Read the passage carefully so that you really understand it, without worrying over the meaning of a few difficult words.
2. Test your reading by asking yourself whether you have formed a definite picture in your mind.
3. While reading, try to find the central idea that lies behind the object, person, or scene described.

Try and apply these rules to the following passage.

[1]

Viewed from the clammy deck on this bright morning, the island of Nepenthe resembled a cloud. It was a silvery speck upon the limitless expanse of blue sea and sky. A south wind breathed over the Mediterranean waters, drawing up their moisture which lay couched in 5 thick mists about its flanks and uplands. The comely outlines were barely suggested through a veil of fog.

An air of irreality hung about the place. Could this be
an island? A veritable island of rocks and vineyards and
houses—this pallid apparition? It looked like some snowy 10
sea-bird resting upon the waves; a sea-bird or a cloud;
one of those lonely clouds that stray from their fellows
and drift about in wayward fashion at the bidding of
every breeze.

NORMAN DOUGLAS
South Wind

Vocabulary

    clammy (l. 1): sticky.
    flanks (l. 6): sides.
    comely (l. 6): pleasant.
    irreality (l. 8): unreality.
    veritable (l. 9): real.
    pallid apparition (l. 10): pale ghost.
    drift about in wayward fashion (l. 13): move about aimlessly
      in a random way.
    bidding (l. 13): command.

The picture you should have formed in your mind is that
of an island seen from a distance ('viewed from the clammy
deck').

The central idea behind the description is that the outline
of the island is still very vague. This idea runs through the
whole piece. Nepenthe is first compared to a cloud, then it
is described as being obscured by a 'veil of fog' so that
even its existence is doubted: to the beholder it is more like
an 'apparition' or 'some snowy sea bird' than an island.
In the last lines, the writer returns to the comparison he
made at the opening: the island is like a drifting cloud.

FINDING THE MEANING

When you have read a passage of descriptive prose carefully, you should be in a position to write its general meaning, its detailed meaning, and give some account of the
writer's intention.

General Meaning. This should be based on a reading of the *whole* passage. You should note the *main object* that is described.

Detailed Meaning. Your account must be accurate and to the point, but as with narrative prose you should not write a précis. Divide the passage into convenient groups where you find that the author is dealing with a new aspect of his subject and give a brief but clear account of each in a single paragraph. When writing the detailed meaning, your aim must be to give the *main characteristics* of what is being described in your own words.

Intention. When writing descriptive prose, an author attempts to re-create something he has seen or imagined. If the description is successful it will always create an atmosphere and convey a central purpose. After grasping the meaning of a piece, it is important to find what the central purpose is if you are to understand the writer's intentions.

Read the passage below and give its general and detailed meaning, and what you consider to be the author's central purpose. When you have done so, compare what you have written with the passage that follows.

[2]

They were entering then the tougher, brighter but darker quay, and passing the fun-fair stood for a moment in the full yellow glare of a large restaurant. This was again a sea-food restaurant—but it was bigger, noisier, brasher, browner, brassier and probably better than   5
those on the other side. Its walls inside were mirrored, its paint and its furniture were of a good weatherbeaten brown, its lights were weak-bulbed and so the yellower, though there were many of them: whereas on the other side of the port carefully printed menus were displayed,   10
here great black slates had been scraped, as if something special had that very moment been cooked or come in, with a brio of chalk: in fact it was a more old-fashioned engine altogether, its yellow glare on to the dark street

was more like the light of a naphtha flare than electric, 15
and it was full, full, full of people crammed together inside
among its mirrors and outside under its huge awning,
all eating fast among waitresses yelling, running and
sometimes if there was time laughing. Plenty of gold in
the teeth of these waitresses, and dark strain beneath 20
their eyes—they touted for customers, beckoning the
street at top-voice, and then had to rush back and serve
them, both making work and doing it.

WILLIAM SANSOM

Question and Answer

Vocabulary

quay (l. 2): a landing-place at the side of which ships can be
tied up.

brasher (l. 5): cruder in a naïve way.

weak-bulbed (l. 8): giving little light.

slates (l. 11): blackboards.

brio (l. 13): flourish. 'Brio' means 'liveliness' and is used in
English as a musical term.

naphtha flare (l. 15): the bright light of an oil-lamp.

crammed (l. 16): crowded.

awning (l. 17): canvas roof used outside a shop to keep off rain
or sun.

touted for customers (l. 21): tried to persuade people to enter.

beckoning (l. 21): inviting.

General meaning, detailed meaning and intention. This is a
description of a restaurant seen by night in the poor and
crowded quarter of a port.

The writer mentions briefly the other section of the port
with its sea-food restaurants displaying printed menus to
point to the striking differences in the big restaurant he
describes here. The menu has been hastily scrawled on
slates; the numerous lights make it appear bright, though
it is not particularly well-lit. The walls inside the building
have been painted brown, the same colour as the furniture,
and are covered with mirrors; outside, there is a huge

awning. The whole place is noisy and packed with people
all eating quickly; waitresses are rushing to serve them
while at the same time shouting to passers-by in an effort
to attract even more customers.

The central idea that runs through the piece is that the
restaurant is an oasis of life and light in the dark streets.
It is a welcoming, friendly place, crowded and vulgar, but
very much alive.

EXERCISES ON FINDING THE MEANING

Answer the questions on the three passages that follow,
bearing in mind the example you have just read.

[3]

I returned to the inn, and went into the kitchen to
speak with the landlady; she had made a hundred hesita-
tions when I told her we wanted three beds. At last she
confessed she *had* three beds, and showed me into a parlour which looked damp and cold, but she assured me in   5
a tone that showed she was unwilling to be questioned
further, that all *her* beds were well aired. I sat a while by
the kitchen fire with the landlady, and began to talk to
her; but, much as I had heard in her praise—for the
shopkeeper had told me she was a varra (very) discreet   10
woman—I cannot say that her manners pleased me
much. But her servant made amends, for she was as
pleasant and cheerful a lass as was ever seen; and when
we asked her to do anything, she answered, 'Oh yes,'
with a merry smile, and almost ran to get us what we   15
wanted. She was about sixteen years old: wore shoes
and stockings, and had her hair tucked up with a
comb. . . . I examined the kitchen round about; it was
crowded with furniture, drawers, cupboards, dish-
covers, pictures, pans and pots, arranged without order,   20
except that the plates were on shelves, and the dish-
covers hung in rows; these were very clean, but floors,
passages, staircase, everything else dirty. There were

two beds in recesses in the wall; above one of them I
noticed a shelf with some books.

DOROTHY WORDSWORTH

Diary

Vocabulary

made amends (l. 12): made up for, compensated.

QUESTIONS

1. How did the parlour appear to the writer?
2. What opinion did the writer form of the landlady?
3. Why did the servant make a favourable impression on the
   writer?
4. State briefly what the writer noticed in the kitchen.
5. Give the general and detailed meaning of the passage and
   what you consider to be the writer's intention.

[4]

There were some birds at night beyond the garden.
Behind their hard cymbal clashes or sad flute sounds I
used to hear the far-away moping of the sea and then the
fitful barking of a dog. I would imagine his cry coming
across the fields, the brimming icy ditches and the bare   5
hedges glittering with black drops of water. Perhaps it
came from some lonely farm where he was chained up
in a cobbled yard. The chain would grate and clink
like a ghost's as he ran from side to side, barking and
waiting for the answer which never came. At last his tail 10
would curve down through his legs and he would huddle
back into the dank straw in his barrel.

DENTON WELCH

A Voice through a Cloud

Vocabulary

cymbal (l. 2): musical instrument consisting of two bronze
plates which are struck together to make a ringing noise.

moping (l. 3): in this sense, melancholy murmur.

fitful barking (l. 4): that which occurred suddenly at irregular intervals.

brimming (l. 5): full to the very top.

cobbled (l. 8): paved with round stones.

the chain would grate and clink (l. 8): i.e., the links of the chain would scrape against one another (*grate*) and make a sharp ringing sound (*clink*).

dank (l. 12): unpleasantly damp.

QUESTIONS

1. What sounds could the writer hear at night?
2. Did the dog really bark or did the writer imagine so?
3. Where did the writer imagine the bark came from?
4. Write the general and detailed meaning of the passage and what you consider to be the writer's intention.

[5]

Mr Squeers' appearance was not prepossessing. He had but one eye, and the popular prejudice runs in favour of two. The eye he had was unquestionably useful, but decidedly not ornamental: being of a greenish grey, and in shape resembling the fan-light of a street 5 door. The blank side of his face was much wrinkled and puckered up, which gave him a very sinister appearance, especially when he smiled, at which times his expression bordered closely on the villainous. His hair was very flat and shiny, save at the ends, where it was 10 brushed stiffly up from a low protruding forehead, which assorted well with his harsh voice and coarse manner. He was about two or three and fifty, and a trifle below the middle size; he wore a white neckerchief with long ends, and a suit of scholastic black; but his coat 15 sleeves being a great deal too long, and his trousers a great deal too short, he appeared ill at ease in his clothes, and as if he were in a perpetual state of astonishment at finding himself so respectable.

CHARLES DICKENS

Nicholas Nickleby

Vocabulary

was not prepossessing (l. 1): did not make a favourable impression.

fan-light (l. 5): rounded window over a door.

puckered up (l. 7): gathered into folds.

bordered closely on (l. 9): closely resembled, was almost.

assorted well with (l. 12): went well with, suited . . . well.

scholastic (l. 15): in this sense, very formal.

ill at ease (l. 17): uncomfortable, not able to feel free and natural.

QUESTIONS

1. Why was Mr Squeers' one eye 'not ornamental'?

2. When did Mr Squeers look 'villainous'?

3. How was Mr Squeers dressed?

4. Does the writer set out simply to describe Mr Squeers in an impartial way? Give reasons for your answer.

5. Give the general and detailed meaning of the passage and what you consider to be the writer's intention.

How it is Done

APPRECIATING DESCRIPTIVE PROSE

When we analyse a good story it is possible to find some of the qualities which make it enjoyable to read. The same can be said for descriptive writing. But in this case, the qualities, or *devices* do not serve the same purpose: describing people, scenes, or objects *for their own sakes* is quite a different thing from telling a story. Appreciation of descriptive writing again involves a study of the *way* a piece has been written.

In the analysis that follows, all the examples have been taken from the passages you have studied.

STRUCTURAL DEVICES

Unity, Contrast, Association.

Unity. When studying the unity of narrative prose you had to observe how everything that happened in the story was essential to the final outcome. In this respect, descriptive prose differs considerably as there is no underlying 'story' to hold it together. It is, therefore, impossible to understand how a piece of descriptive writing is held together unless you first discern the central purpose that underlies it.

In the passage from *South Wind*, the author's central purpose is to describe an island which cannot be clearly seen. Everything that follows, the likening of the island to a cloud, to a bird and to an apparition, together with the description of the fog, contributes to this purpose, so that not a single word in the paragraph is irrelevant. Notice, too, how the opening and final sentences are linked together: in both the island is compared to a cloud.

William Sansom in the passage from *Question and Answer* creates the lively atmosphere of a busy restaurant as it is seen at night in the poorer quarter of a port. He intends to show that the restaurant, for all its vulgarity, is bright and friendly. The descriptions of the walls, furniture, mirrors, lights, waitresses and crowds are all closely related to each other in that they are essential to the atmosphere of the restaurant and they serve to make the picture very complete indeed.

The passage from *A Voice through a Cloud* differs from the others you have read: here the writer describes what he imagined rather than what he saw. The whole piece is built round the barking of a dog. The writer imagines the way the sound has travelled over 'icy ditches' from a lonely farm until he reaches the dog itself: barking, waiting for an answer that never comes, and finally retiring to its kennel. The writer's purpose is to trace the source of the sound and this idea runs through the whole passage.

Dickens' intention in the passage from *Nicholas Nickleby* is to describe Squeers while at the same time showing him to be an unpleasant person. To do this he links moral and physical attributes. Squeers' ugly appearance reflects his equally ugly character. His voice is harsh, his smile 'villainous'; his clothes respectable, while he is not, so that he is 'ill at ease'. Every detail in this piece contributes to the writer's double purpose.

Contrast always gives added interest and colour to the object that is being described.

Notice the briefly drawn contrast in *Question and Answer*. The restaurants on the other side of the port are well-lit and display well-printed menus: by comparison, the restaurant that is described is 'a more old-fashioned engine altogether'. But the writer implies that the other side of the port is staid and unattractive, whereas the 'old engine' is 'full, full, full of people crammed together'.

Dorothy Wordsworth's description of the inn in her *Diary* is made all the more lively by her account of the people there. The unpleasant landlady is contrasted with the cheerful servant girl.

The contrast in the passage from *Nicholas Nickleby* is very much more subtle. Mr Squeers' respectable clothes are in conflict with his villainous character. The contrast is made even more telling when we are informed that the clothes do not fit him: 'his coat sleeves being a great deal too long, and his trousers a great deal too short'.

Association. This occurs when, in the course of describing an object, a writer is reminded of something else. An author may sometimes fix our attention on one object and then go on to describe it in an oblique way by referring to another.

A good example of this occurs in *South Wind*. The island itself is not really described at all: it is so vague in outline that it suggests a cloud. The cloud suggests an apparition and then a seabird. In the final lines, the author returns to the image of the cloud, 'one of those lonely clouds that stray from their fellows'. But it is not a cloud he is writing about: it is the island of Nepenthe. This oblique method of description emphasizes the hazy, indistinct character of the island.

The passage from *A Voice through a Cloud* is likewise built up by means of association. First there are three sounds: those of the birds, the sea and the dog. The author concentrates on the last and takes us on an imaginary journey across fields, ditches and hedges to a lonely farm where we come upon the dog itself. In this way, beginning with an apparently meaningless bark, the writer constructs a whole descriptive scene and leads the reader from one image to another.

SENSE DEVICES

Style, Use of words, Metaphor, Simile.

Style. The way a writer expresses himself depends largely on the nature of the object he is describing and the atmosphere he is trying to create. The writer's central purpose dictates the style to be employed.

You will have observed how simple and direct the writing is in Dorothy Wordsworth's *Diary*. At the same time the writer pays considerable attention to detail and makes minute and exact observations. Notice especially how in the last few lines ('I examined the kitchen . . .') all the facts noted are expressed in a plain, orderly way. By comparison with this, the style in *Question and Answer* is much more elaborate. Here the writer does not simply want us to *see* the restaurant: he wants us to hear the noise round about and make us feel that we, too, are part of the crowd. Although the passage is packed with detail, there is none of the dispassionate reporting we find in the *Diary* because the author's aim is quite different. The brown walls and furniture, the mirrors, the people, the garish light and noise, together with unexpected details ('Plenty of gold in the teeth of those waitresses'), all coming on top of one another, make the reader feel that he is taking an active part in what is happening and is not simply an observer. The same attention to detail and effort to create atmosphere is to be found in *A Voice through a Cloud*. The reader is carefully led, as it were, backwards from the bark to the dog, lingering at each place over which the sound has travelled.

In both *Nicholas Nickleby* and *South Wind*, the writers' attention to detail has a different purpose. In the former, Dickens does not only want us to *see* Squeers but to disapprove of him and so combines exact description with reprobation. In the latter, Norman Douglas deliberately sets out to confuse us: is that really an island in the distance? Or is it a cloud, a bird or an apparition? The impression we have of the island after reading the passage is vague: the island is as remote as ever—as it is meant to be.

When examining the style of any particular piece, always observe how the writer handles detail and notice whether you are required to see an object as an observer or to take part in what is being described.

Use of words, Metaphor, Simile. All good descriptive writing aims at enabling the reader to share the writer's experience. It follows, therefore, that if a writer is to make his description come alive in such a way that it will have an immediate impact on the reader, he must avoid using commonplace words and hackneyed expressions: care in the choice of words becomes all-important.

In *South Wind*, notice how the word 'clammy', describing the hot and sticky deck, contrasts with the unearthly 'silvery speck' in the distance. Further on, the metaphor 'pallid apparition' and the similes 'like some snowy sea-bird' and 'one of those lonely clouds' suggest vividly that the island can hardly be real. The phrases are so carefully chosen that they heighten our impression of the distant island.

In the same way the harsh barking of a dog in *A Voice through a Cloud* contrasts with the metaphors used to describe bird-song: 'cymbal clashes' and 'sad flute sounds'. The vividly described details that follow oblige the reader to linger at the places over which the sound has travelled: 'brimming icy ditches' and hedges 'glittering with black drops of water'. When we reach the dog itself its imaginary

chain 'grates and clinks' so that we can almost hear it.
The words 'huddle back' suggest the dog's disappointment
at receiving no answer.

Words are brilliantly handled in *Question and Answer*
where the author attempts to convey many impressions at
once. By using carefully chosen adjectives he is able to
paint whole scenes in single phrases: 'tougher, brighter but
darker quay' and 'noisier, brasher, browner, brassier . . .'
This general picture is filled out later as the description
develops: the walls are a 'weatherbeaten brown', the slates
scraped with 'a brio of chalk'. The scene is then summed up
in the metaphor: 'It was a more old fashioned engine altogether.' When the crowds are described, the writer again
gives us a general picture with the repeated word 'full'
('it was full, full, full of people'). The impression that there
are people everywhere is enhanced by the way the waitresses
tout for customers 'beckoning the street'. In almost every
line in the passage the careful choice of words helps re-
create the dazzling scene described.

Turn back to the passages from the *Diary* and *Nicholas
Nickleby* and comment on the vocabulary used.

EXERCISES ON APPRECIATION

[1]

The yard was now in daylight, a greyish light tinged
with yellow, not unfriendly, promising more snow. It
was about eight—only three hours had passed since he
first entered the cell. The walls surrounding the yard
looked like those of barracks; iron gates were in front of   5
all the windows, the cells behind them were too dark
for one to see into them. It was impossible even to see
whether anyone stood directly behind his window, looking down, like him at the snow in the yard. It was nice
snow, slightly frozen; it would crackle if one walked on   10
it. On both sides of the path which ran round the yard
at a distance of ten paces from the walls, a hilly parapet
of snow had been shovelled up. On the rampart opposite

the sentinel was pacing up and down. Once, when turn- ing, he spat in a wide arc into the snow; then leant over 15 the ramp to see where it had fallen and frozen.

ARTHUR KOESTLER

Darkness at Noon

Vocabulary

> parapet (l. 12): mound, low wall.
> rampart (l. 13): long defensive mound.
> sentinel (l. 14): guard.

QUESTIONS

1. Give the general and detailed meaning of the passage and what you consider to be the writer's intention.
2. In what way do the details given bring out the writer's central purpose?
3. Comment briefly on the writer's style and choice of words.

[2]

A stout man with a pink face wears dingy white flannel trousers, a blue coat with a pink handkerchief showing, and a straw hat much too small for him, perched at the back of his head. He plays the guitar. A little chap in white canvas shoes, his face hidden under a felt 5 hat like a broken wing, breathes into a flute; and a tall thin fellow, with bursting over-ripe button boots, draws ribbons—long, twisted, streaming ribbons—of tune out of a fiddle. They stand, unsmiling, but not serious, in the broad sunlight opposite the fruit-shop; the pink 10 spider of a hand beats the guitar, the little squat hand, with a brass-and-turquoise ring, forces the reluctant flute, and the fiddler's arm tries to saw the fiddle in two.

KATHERINE MANSFIELD

The Garden Party

Vocabulary

dingy (l. 1): dirty-looking.
fiddle (l. 9): violin.
squat (l. 11): short and thick, not long as a musician's is
    supposed to be.

QUESTIONS

1. Give the general and detailed meaning of the passage and
   what you consider to be the writer's intention.
2. Comment on the way the paragraph has been constructed.
3. Would you say the writer is attentive to detail? Give reasons
   for your answer.
4. Find a simile and two metaphors in the passage, and say what
   they do.
5. Explain the effect of 'dingy' (l. 1); 'bursting over-ripe button
   boots' (l. 7); 'draws ribbons' (ll. 7–8); 'the pink spider'
   (ll. 10–11); 'the little squat hand' (l. 11); 'reluctant flute'
   (ll. 12–13).

[3]

I can see now, of course, that he didn't really like me.
It was not the poor man's fault. He had never expected
to be the father of a genius and it filled him with fore-
bodings. He looked round him at all his contemporaries
who had normal, bloodthirsty, illiterate children, and   5
shuddered at the thought that I would never be good
for anything but being a genius. To give him his due,
it wasn't himself he worried about, but he dreaded the
shame of it. He would come in from the front door with
his cap over his eyes and his hands in his trousers   10
pockets and stare moodily at me while I sat at the
kitchen table, surrounded by papers, producing fresh
maps and illustrations for my book of voyages, or copy-
ing the music of 'The Minstrel Boy'.

FRANK O'CONNOR
Domestic Relations

Vocabulary

> forebodings (ll. 3–4): feelings that something evil would occur.
> to give him his due (l. 7): to be fair to him.

QUESTIONS

1. Give the general and detailed meaning of the passage and what you consider to be the writer's intention.
2. Explain how the details given bring out the writer's central purpose.
3. How is the boy contrasted (a) with his father, (b) with other children?
4. Comment on the use of the word 'genius'.

Literary Appreciation

Your written appreciation of the passages at the end of this Chapter should be in continuous prose and you must take every care to show how the devices you find in them bring out the writer's central purpose and contribute to the atmosphere he creates.

The substance of this Chapter is summarized below as a key to remind you of what you have to look for when appreciating descriptive prose.

KEY

1. READING	Form a definite picture in your mind; look for a central purpose.
2. MEANING	*General* *Detailed*: the main characteristics. *Intention*: the central idea.
3. DEVICES	
(a) STRUCTURAL	*Unity*: how everything contributes to the central idea. *Contrast* *Association*
(b) SENSE	*Style* Use of Words, metaphor, simile.

E

The passage that follows is a full appreciation of *Question and Answer* by William Sansom. Study it carefully before attempting to write appreciation of your own and note how it has been written.

This is a description of a restaurant seen by night in the poor and crowded quarter of a port.

The writer mentions briefly the other section of the port with its sea-food restaurants displaying printed menus to point to the striking differences in the big restaurant he describes here. The menu has been hastily scrawled on slates; the numerous lights make it appear bright, though it is not particularly well-lit. The walls inside the building have been painted brown, the same colour as the furniture and are covered with mirrors; outside, there is a huge awning. The whole place is noisy and packed with people all eating quickly; waitresses are rushing to serve them while at the same time shouting to passers-by in an effort to attract even more customers.

The central idea that runs through the piece is that the restaurant is an oasis of life and light in the dark streets. It is a welcoming, friendly place, crowded and vulgar, but very much alive.

After the writer has led us into the 'brighter but darker quay' and confronted us with the sea-food restaurant, he gives a brief general description of the scene: the place is big, noisy, brash, and brown. The writer completes this general picture by amplifying each of these qualities. The walls and furniture are 'a good weatherbeaten brown'; the numerous weak-bulbed lights, the mirrors and slates, make the restaurant appear 'brash'; the impression of noise is conveyed by the crowds 'crammed together' and by the waitresses rushing to serve them and yelling 'at top-voice'.

The liveliness of the scene is further emphasized by the writer's brief references to the restaurants on 'the other side of the port' which are well-lit and 'respectable' but are (it is implied) staid and unattractive. This contrast is briefly drawn but it serves to make the writer's colourful picture all the more vivid.

The nature of the scene described obliges the writer to adopt a difficult style. His intention here is not to give us a plain, matter-of-fact account of what he has seen, but to make us actually hear and feel all that is going on. The author achieves this by giving us arresting details like 'black slates had been scraped . . . with a brio of chalk' or 'plenty of gold in the teeth of these waitresses'.

The author's gift for choosing apt words and phrases makes the scene he describes exciting to read. The adjectives 'tougher, brighter but darker' describing the quay and the list that follows: 'noisier, brasher, browner, brassier . . .' give us a compact, overall impression of the scene. Unusual phrases like 'weatherbeaten brown', 'weakbulbed', 'naphtha flare' and 'beckoning the street' arrest and hold our attention. The very striking metaphor 'old-fashioned engine' at once suggests that the place is noisy. By means of his skilful handling of words the writer has re-created a dazzling scene and brought it to life for the reader.

Write an appreciation of each of the passages that follow.

[1]

A hundred miles, north, south, east, west. Thirty thousand square miles of unbroken cloud-plains! No traveller in the desert, no pioneer to the poles had ever seen such an expanse of sand or snow. Only the lonely threshers of the sky, hidden from the earth, had gazed 5 on it. Only we who went up into the high places under the shadow of wings!

I sailed on for a time, alone in the wonderful skies, as happy as I have ever been or ever shall be, I suppose, in this life, looking lazily for some rift in the white 10 floor; but there was none. It was complete, unbroken, absolute. I was about to turn west again when I saw, in the distance, a cloud floating above the floor, small, no bigger than a man's hand; but even as I looked, it

seemed to grow. It swelled, budded, massed, and I 15
realized that I was watching the very birth of a cloud—
the cumulus cloud that chiefly makes the glory of the
sky, the castles, battlements, cathedrals of the heavens.
What laws had governed its birth at that moment, at
that place, amid the long savannahs of the blue? Heaven, 20
that bore it, knew. Still it was there, creating a growing
loveliness out of nothing! a marriage of light and water,
fostered by the sun, nourished by the sky!

I turned towards it, fascinated. It grew rapidly. Soon
it was vast, towering, magnificent, its edges sharp, 25
seemingly solid, though constantly swelling and changing. And it was alive with light. Radiant white, satin
soft, and again gold, rose-tinted, shadowed and graded
into blue and mauve shadows—an orient pearl in the
oyster shell of heaven! And all the time I knew that I 30
had but to come close enough for all the illusion to be
gone, the solidity and beauty to dissolve, the edges to
fray and dull, and that within it would be the same grey
mist that you may meet on any moor in England.

CECIL LEWIS

Sagittarius Rising

Vocabulary

threshers of the sky (l. 5): i.e., those who repeatedly fly.
rift (l. 10): crack.
budded (l. 15): grew.
cumulous cloud (l. 17): type of cloud which forms in rounded
    masses.
battlements (l. 18): indented walls around a fortress.
savannahs (l. 20): great stretches of grass-land without trees.
fostered by the sun (l. 23): i.e., the sun helped it to grow.
to fray (ll. 32–3): to become torn and uneven.

[2]

But though I was terrified by the idea of the seafaring
man with one leg, I was far less afraid of the captain
himself than anybody else who knew him. There were

nights when he took a deal more rum and water than his
head would carry; and then he would sometimes sit and 5
sing his wicked, old, wild sea-songs, minding nobody;
but sometimes he would call for glasses round, and
force all the trembling company to listen to his stories
or bear a chorus to his singing. Often I have heard the
house shaking with 'Yo-ho-ho, and a bottle of rum'; all 10
the neighbours joining in for dear life, with the fear of
death upon them, and each singing louder than the
other, to avoid remark. For in these fits he was the most
overriding companion ever known; he would slap his
hand on the table for silence all round; he would fly up 15
in a passion of anger at a question, or sometimes because
none was put, and so he judged the company was not
following his story. Nor would he allow anyone to leave
the inn till he had drunk himself sleepy and reeled off to
bed. 20

His stories were what frightened people worst of all.
Dreadful stories they were; about hanging, and walking
the plank, and storms at sea and the Dry Tortugas, and
wild deeds and places on the Spanish Main. By his own
account he must have lived his life among some of the 25
wickedest men that God ever allowed upon the sea; and
the language in which he told these stories shocked our
plain country people almost as much as the crimes he
described. My father was always saying the inn would
be ruined, for people would soon cease coming there to 30
be tyrannized over and put down, and sent shivering to
their beds; but I really believe his presence did us good.
People were frightened at the time, but on looking back
they rather liked it; it was a fine excitement in a quiet
country life; and there was even a party of the younger 35
men who pretended to admire him, calling him a 'true
sea-dog,' and a 'real old salt,' and such-like names, and
saying there was the sort of man that made England
terrible at sea.

ROBERT LOUIS STEVENSON

Treasure Island

Vocabulary

he would call for glasses round (l. 7): he would buy drinks
for everybody.

to avoid remark (l. 13): to escape notice.

fits (l. 13): sudden outbursts.

reeled off (l. 19): walked unsteadily.

walking the plank (ll. 22–3): being made to walk blindfold along
a board and into the sea. (Pirates sometimes made their
prisoners do this.)

a real old salt (l. 37): a sailor who has had long experience of
the sea.

[3]

He was not rich; although his income, in those days,
allowed the preservation of a fairly independent attitude
towards the more material side of being an artist. He had
once, for example, turned down the opportunity to
decorate the interior of a fish restaurant in Brighton—   5
where he lived—on grounds that the sum offered was
incommensurate with the demeaning nature of the work
demanded. His means had also enabled him to assemble
what was said to be an excellent little collection of hour-
glasses, silhouettes, and bric-à-brac of various kinds.   10
At the same time he liked to describe how, from time to
time, in order to avoid the expense and responsibility of
domestic staff, he deliberately underwent long periods
of undertaking his own cooking. 'I could always earn
my living as a chef,' he used to say; adding, in joke,   15
that he would look 'enormously ornamental' in a white
cap. When travelling on the Continent he commonly
went on foot with a haversack on his back, rather than
by trains, which he found 'stuffy and infinitely filled
with tedious persons'. He was careful, even rather fussy,   20
about his health, especially in relation to personal clean-
liness and good sanitation; so that some of the more
sordid aspects of these allegedly *terre-à-terre* excursions
abroad must at times have been a trial to him. Perhaps
his Continental visits were, in fact, more painful for   25

managers of hotels and restaurants frequented by him;
for he was a great believer in insisting absolutely upon
the minute observance by others of his own wishes.
Such habits of travelling, in so much as they were
indeed voluntary and not to some degree enforced by 30
financial consideration, were no doubt also connected in
his mind with his own special approach to social behaviour, in which he was guided by an aversion, often
expressed, for conduct that might be looked upon either
as conventional or conservative.   35

ANTHONY POWELL
A Buyer's Market

Vocabulary

turned down (l. 4): refused.
incommensurate (l. 7): inadequate, not enough.
demeaning (l. 7): undignified.
silhouettes(l. 10): portraits in solid black and white giving out-
    lines only.
bric-à-brac (l. 10): curiosities; small ornaments.
allegedly (l. 23): which were supposed to have taken place.
terre-à-terre (l. 23): undignified, commonplace.
aversion (l. 33): dislike.
conventional (l. 35): ordinary, in accordance with custom.
conservative (l. 35): cautious.

[4]

On January 21, around noon, our plane took off from
New York. It was nearly dark when we reached New-
foundland and circled over the snow-woods and the
frozen lakes to Gander, a tiny sprinkle of lights in the
wilderness. Transatlantic air travel was somewhat more 5
of an adventure in those days, and less elegantly con-
ducted. The big bare white waiting-hall, with its table
of simple refreshments, seemed very much a frontier-
post; here were the last cup of coffee and the last bun in
the Western Hemisphere.   10
I didn't sleep at all, that night. Not because I was

unduly nervous; it was rather a kind of awe that kept me awake. If you are old enough, as I am, to remember Blériot—not to mention Lindbergh—it seems incredible to find yourself actually flying the Atlantic. I sat at my 15 little window with its doll's house curtains, vibrating with the changing rhythms of the aircraft and peering out for glimpses of the stars. Fragments of ice, dislodged from the wings, kept rattling against the pane. The cabin was dark, except for a few pin-rays of light 20 from overhead reading lamps. Although all the seats around me were occupied, I felt curiously alone—for the journey I was making was back through time rather than forward through space, and it concerned no one on board except myself. 25

And then—in palest saffron, in pink, in scarlet, in stabbing gold—the sunrise. It gleamed dully on our wet metal and on the cloud field below us, which was blue-grey like dirty snow. We were flying over an arctic aerial landscape; weirdly solid, with terraces, erosions, 30 valleys and great rounded rugged hills. The roar of our engines, which had been so loud through the night, now sank, or seemed to sink, to a soft hushing sigh. We were gradually coming lower. The plane skimmed the cloud-drifts like a motor-boat, and you had a sudden 35 terrific sense of speed and impact, as though it would surely be dashed to pieces. We raced over them, through them, with the thick vapour whirling back in shreds from our propellers, massing, towering above us, bursting upon us in furious silent breakers. Then, through a 40 wide rift, we saw Ireland—a country of bogs and stony fields, green and mournful in the showery morning, crossed by the winding estuary of the Shannon.

CHRISTOPHER ISHERWOOD

Coming to London

Vocabulary

a tiny sprinkle of lights (l. 4): a few lights scattered here and there.

bun (l. 9): a kind of round sweet cake.

fragments (l. 18): pieces.

dislodged (ll. 18–19): broke away.

saffron (l. 26): orange colour.

stabbing (l. 27): in this sense, striking, dazzling.

weirdly (l. 30): peculiarly.

erosions (l. 30): here in the sense of 'cracks'.

skimmed (l. 34): went over the top, almost touching.

sense of . . . impact (l. 36): feeling that you were hitting into something.

whirling (l. 38): going round and round quickly.

shreds (l. 38): ragged streamers.

breakers (l. 40): waves.

bogs (l. 41): wet spongy ground.

estuary (l. 43): river-mouth.

[5]

We had visiting us at this time a nervous first cousin of mine name Briggs Beall, who believed that he was likely to cease breathing when he was asleep. It was his feeling that if he were not awakened every hour during the night, he might die of suffocation. He had been 5 accustomed to setting an alarm clock to ring at intervals until morning, but I persuaded him to abandon this. He slept in my room and I told him that I was such a light sleeper that if anybody quit breathing in the same room with me, I would wake instantly. He tested me the first 10 night—which I had suspected he would—by holding his breath after my regular breathing had convinced him I was asleep. I was not asleep, however, and called to him. This seemed to allay his fears a little, but he took the precaution of putting a glass of spirits of camphor on 15 a little table at the head of his bed. In case I didn't arouse him until he was almost gone, he said, he would sniff the camphor, a powerful reviver. Briggs was not the only member of his family who had his crotchets. Old Aunt Melissa Beall (who could whistle like a man, with 20 two fingers in her mouth) suffered under the premonition that she was destined to die on South High Street, because she had been born on South High Street and married on South High Street. Then there was Aunt Sarah Shoaf, who never went to bed at night without 25 the fear that a burglar was going to get in and blow chloroform under her door through a tube. To avert this calamity—for she was in greater dread of anaesthetics than of losing her household goods—she always piled her money, silverware, and other valuables in a 30 neat stack just outside her bedroom, with a note reading: 'This is all I have. Please take it and do not use your chloroform, as this is all I have.' Aunt Gracie Shoaf also had a burglar phobia, but she met it with more fortitude. She was confident that burglars had 35 been getting into her house every night for forty years. The fact that she never missed anything was to her no proof to the contrary. She always claimed that she scared them off before they could take anything, by throwing shoes down the hallway. When she went to 40 bed she piled, where she could get at them handily, all the shoes there were about her house. Five minutes after she had turned off the light, she would sit up in bed and say 'Hark!' Her husband, who had learned to ignore the whole situation as long ago as 1903, would either be 45 sound asleep or pretend to be sound asleep. In either case he would not respond to her tugging and pulling, so that presently she would arise, tiptoe to the door, open it slightly and heave a shoe down the hall in one direction, and its mate down the hall in the other direc- 50 tion. Some nights she threw them all, some nights only a couple of pairs.

JAMES THURBER

My Life and Hard Times

Vocabulary

suffocation (l. 5): inability to breathe.

quit (l. 9): stopped.

to allay his fears (l. 14): to make him feel less afraid.

camphor (l. 15): a white, strong-smelling substance used as a medicine.

crotchets (l. 19): unreasonable ideas.

premonition (ll. 21-2): forewarning, a feeling that something evil will happen.

avert this calamity (ll. 27-8): avoid this disaster.

anaesthetics (ll. 28-9): drugs which cause one to lose consciousness.

stack (l. 31): pile.

phobia (l. 34): fear.

handily (l. 41): easily.

hark (l. 44): listen.

heave (l. 49): throw.

[6]

The sun had not yet risen. The sea was indistinguishable from the sky, except that the sea was slightly creased as if a cloth had wrinkles in it. Gradually as the sky whitened a dark line lay on the horizon dividing the sea from the sky and the grey cloth became barred with thick strokes 5 moving, one after another, beneath the surface, following each other, pursuing each other, perpetually.

As they neared the shore each bar rose, heaped itself, broke and swept a thin veil of white water across the sand. The wave paused, and then drew out again, sigh- 10 ing like a sleeper whose breath comes and goes unconsciously. Gradually the dark bar on the horizon became clear as if the sediment in an old wine-bottle had sunk and left the glass green. Behind it, too, the sky cleared as if the white sediment there had sunk, or as if 15 the arm of a woman couched beneath the horizon had raised a lamp and flat bars of white, green and yellow spread across the sky like the blades of a fan. Then she raised her lamp higher and the air seemed to become fibrous and to tear away from the green surface flicker- 20 ing and flaming in red and yellow fibres like the smoky fire that roars from a bonfire. Gradually the fibres of the

burning bonfire were fused into one haze, one incandescence which lifted the weight of the woollen grey sky
on top of it and turned it to a million atoms of soft blue. 25
The surface of the sea slowly became transparent and
lay rippling and sparkling until the dark stripes were
almost rubbed out. Slowly the arm that held the lamp
raised it higher and then higher until a broad flame
became visible; an arc of fire burnt on the rim of the 30
horizon, and all round it the sea blazed gold.

VIRGINIA WOOLF

The Waves

Vocabulary

barred (l. 5): marked with lines.

sediment (l. 15): matter that settles at the bottom of a liquid.

seemed . . . fibrous (ll. 19–20): seemed as though it were
made up of threads (fibres).

flickering (ll. 20–1): burning unsteadily.

bonfire (l. 23): a large fire made out of doors with leaves, etc.

fused (l. 23): joined.

incandescence (ll. 23–4): intense brightness.

8

ARGUMENT
What is it About?

HOW TO READ ARGUMENTATIVE PROSE

The most difficult type of prose to read is that which deals with ideas and facts. When reading a story or a description, it is relatively easy to visualize what is going on: we *see* and *imagine* rather than *think*. Because argumentative prose requires us to think, it needs to be read two or three times (and sometimes more) if it is to be understood fully. Furthermore, since each sentence logically adds something to the argument, your reading must be very attentive.

The way to go about reading argument may be summed up as follows:

1. Read the passage as many times as you feel it is necessary for you to understand it fully.

2. While reading, make sure you have a clear idea what it is the writer is arguing about.

3. As far as you can, notice how everything the writer says contributes to his main argument.

Now see how far you can put these rules into effect when reading the following passage.

[1]

The status of the author is not what it was. Society, as people say, takes a dimmer view of him than it used to do. Possibly authors themselves are not what they were. It is an argument easy to use, and we often meet it. But it misses the point, even if we are now nothing but so   5 many scribbling midgets. If there arose among us a

young novelist who was a greater genius than the
Dickens of the Early Victorian period, he could never
triumphantly capture the country as Dickens did. He
would face too much competition, not merely from   10
other books but from TV, radio, films; there would not
be sufficient attention and excitement to spare to afford
him his triumph; the public of today would not co-
operate as the Victorians did. (In passing, let me add
that it has long been my view that a deep-seated and   15
passionate public need has an immediate effect upon any
form of art. This explains the astonishing development
of Elizabethan drama, the 19th-century novel, and even
the silent film, which between 1910–1925 made amazing
progress.) We can bring this nearer home. The public   20
now would not co-operate as it was doing even in the
'twenties and early 'thirties. At the present time it does
not want to create this particular sort of reputation, with
the result that no such reputations are made. During
the last ten years the flood of new books has been in full   25
spate, but where among the new writers are those whose
names are now household words? We have our post-war
public figures, but how many of them are authors?

J. B. PRIESTLEY

The Future of the Writer

Vocabulary

status (l. 1): position; rank.

takes a dimmer view of him (l. 2): thinks less of him.

scribbling midgets (l. 6): small, unimportant people writing
      hurriedly and carelessly.

TV (l. 11): television.

has been in full spate (ll. 25–6): (spate: river-flood), i.e., they
      have appeared in ever-increasing numbers.

household words (l. 27): i.e., familiar to everybody.

If you have read the passage carefully you will have
noticed that the writer's main argument is that an author's
position in society is not what it used to be.

This idea is expressed in the opening sentence and is developed and explained in all that follows. The writer begins by dismissing an argument that is 'easy to use', namely, that it is the author's fault and not that of society, that a writer's position is not what it was. A great novelist writing today, he says, would have less success than Dickens had because in our time books have to compete with other means of entertainment. The next point the writer makes, even though it is an 'aside' contributes greatly to his main argument: the popularity of an art-form in any age helps its development. Following up this argument the writer concludes by saying that even though a great many books are published today, writing as an art-form is less popular and therefore few authors enjoy a big reputation.

Notice how every point the writer makes drives home his main argument.

FINDING THE MEANING

You can only be in a position to give the general and detailed meaning and to state the intentions of a writer when you have read his argument attentively.

General Meaning. (a) If the argument is contained in a single paragraph, the general meaning will often be found in the opening sentence—what is called the 'topic sentence'. (b) If the argument is contained in more than one paragraph, the general meaning will be found in the opening paragraph.

In each case it is necessary to read the *whole* passage to find the general meaning as an author may sometimes deal with *more than one* important topic in his argument. When you are sure you have understood what the general meaning is, you should re-state it in your own words in a single sentence.

Detailed Meaning. Any argument, if it is to be convincing, is built very gradually and each point is either proved by reference to facts or logically deduced from what has gone before. Thus, there are always definite stages in any argumentative passage. In your final reading of a piece, it is a good idea to divide it up into what you consider to be its main stages. In this way you can give the important points contained in each stage in a single paragraph. Remember, you are *not* writing a précis, but simply recounting the *main stages* of the argument in your own words as accurately as you can. You must take care not to add your own ideas to those of the writer, or to twist his meaning so that it will conform with your own particular notions.

Intention. Argument can take many forms. An author may simply give an account of a problem and leave it unsolved because there is no solution, or he may give a great number of solutions. He may actively try to persuade you to believe something or simply give you his own personal view of a problem without trying to persuade you at all.

Before you can appreciate argumentative prose, it is absolutely necessary to have a clear picture in your mind of the writer's intentions. Is the writer simply giving an account of a problem? Is the problem solved? Is the writer trying to persuade you? Is the argument convincing? Is the writer simply putting over his own private viewpoint?

Read the passage below and give its general and detailed meaning. Then try and decide what the writer's intentions are. Compare what you have written with the passage that follows.

[2]

The art of persuading, exemplified in advertisements, in the lay-out of newspapers, and in the modes of selecting news that are practised by journalists, cannot be entirely neglected by a public speaker who aims at moving his audience to do something. The speaker must 5
attract the attention of his audience, and he must, further, so hold their interest that they will continue to listen to him. Accordingly, he must enforce what he has to say by the method of repetition with variety of expression, since it is not easy to grasp any complicated 10
matter at first hearing. Finally, he must make his

hearers feel that he has a right to be addressing them. For this purpose, he must claim to speak with some measure of authority. In the fulfilment of these needs lie great temptations for the speaker and grave dangers for the audience. If a speaker were to announce that he had no special competence in the problem to be discussed, if he were resolutely to refuse to make any point more than once, if he were to refrain from making any appeal to the emotional attitudes of his hearers, then they would become bored and inattentive. In that case the speaker might just as well stand silent in front of his audience. This, you will notice, would be a contradiction in terms. An effective speaker will gauge the response of his hearers. Some audiences deserve the speakers who exploit their suggestibility and ignorance.

L. SUSAN STEBBING

Thinking to some Purpose

Vocabulary

layout of newspapers (l. 2): the way news is arranged on the pages.

competence (l. 17): ability, special knowledge.

a contradiction in terms (ll. 23–4): a statement containing words that contradict each other (i.e. l. 22, the *speaker* might . . . *stand silent*).

gauge . . . his hearers (ll. 24–5): will find out exactly how his audience feels about him.

General meaning, detailed meaning and intention. The writer analyses the way a speaker should persuade an audience into believing something and points out some of the dangers involved in the fulfilment of this purpose.

What the writer first considers is *how* a speaker should address an audience. A speaker, she says, should keep his hearers interested, repeat himself to make his points clear, avoid expressing himself in a monotonous way, and speak with an air of authority. The necessity for such tactics gives rise to dangers for both the speaker and his audience. The danger for a speaker is that he will fail to persuade his hearers if he ignores these precepts and makes no appeal to emotion. On the other hand, a speaker may abuse the means of persuasion at his disposal and thus get his audience to believe anything he says.

The writer's intention is to make us think about the problems involved in public speaking and the dangers that face both a speaker and his audience.

EXERCISES ON FINDING THE MEANING

Answer the questions on the three passages that follow, bearing in mind the example you have just read.

[3]

Just as it is vital for parents to live their own lives as fully as possible and to deepen their understanding of themselves to the utmost, so is it important for teachers and educators to do the same. When children go to school their teachers become, during school hours, sub- 5
stitutes for the parents, the children transfer to the teacher some of the feelings they have for their parents and are influenced in their turn by the personalities of the teachers. This mutual relationship is of more importance than any teaching method, and a child's ability to 10
learn is continually hampered if the relationship is un-
satisfactory. Again, if teachers really want to be educators, to help children to develop into satisfactory men and women, and not simply to 'stuff them with knowledge', they will only be really successful if they themselves 15
have sound personalities. No amount of preaching, how-
ever well done, no principles, however sound, no clever technique or mechanical aids can replace the influence of a well-developed personality.

FRIEDA FORDHAM

Psychology and Education
(From *An Introduction to Jung's Psychology*)

Vocabulary

> to the utmost (l. 3): as much as possible.
> mutual relationship (l. 9): a relationship in which both the child and the teacher have an effect on each other.
> hampered (l. 11): hindered.

QUESTIONS

1. Why, according to the writer, is it important for teachers to 'deepen their understanding of themselves'? (ll. 2-3).

2. 'This mutual relationship . . .' (l. 9): Which relationship?

3. What is the writer's view of clever teaching techniques?

4. What different meanings does the writer attach to the terms 'teacher' and 'educator'?

5. Write the general and detailed meaning of the passage and what you consider to be the writer's intention.

[4]

In everyday speech, we talk of having a good memory, of having a poor memory, of having a better memory for faces than for names, of having a memory that is failing, and so on. Such talk suggests that memory is an object, a thing which we possess in the same way as we possess 5
a head or a big toe. Yet it is true, although alarming, to say that there is no such thing as memory. A big toe can be seen and touched, but not so memory. Should an acquaintance boast of having an excellent memory, we cannot confirm his claim in the same way as if he boasted 10
the possession of a well-stocked library. We cannot ask him to show us his memory. What we could do, however, is to let him read the page of a book, then have him close the book and try to recite what he has just read. If he reels off the page verbatim, we conclude that 15
his claim, is, at the least, not without foundation. But we have not observed anything which could be called a memory. We have given him an opportunity to learn something and then to demonstrate how well he remembers it. We have not examined anything which he has, 20

but have watched him doing something, namely, repeating or trying to repeat something he has read. In short,
we have concerned ourselves not with an object but with
an activity, not with his memory but with his activity
of remembering.   25

I. M. L. HUNTER
Memory

Vocabulary

    reels off (l. 15): recites effortlessly.
    verbatim (l. 15): word for word.

QUESTIONS

1. What does popular talk about memory lead us to believe?
2. What example does the writer give to support the statement
   that 'there is no such thing as memory'? (l. 7).
3. How does the writer distinguish between the terms 'memory'
   and 'remembering'?
4. Write the general and detailed meaning of the passage and
   what you consider to be the writer's intention.

[5]

The quality of an artist's vision has no other limit
than the imaginative equipment of the artist himself.
Whatever the human eye is capable of observing or the
human mind of conceiving is the potential raw material
for the work of art. But the limitations of the medium   5
are definite and physical. What the dancer can express
is circumscribed by what his body can achieve in the
way of movement. He is bound by the law of gravity, the
nature of human anatomy and the behaviour of his
muscular equipment. Each medium has its own inherent   10
limitations, and potentialities. The artist as craftsman
must accept those limitations, and by accepting, exploit
them. For the sculptor, each of the materials at his disposal—marble, stone, clay, wax, or metal—has its own
way of behaving; each responds to the artist's control of 15

them by controlling him in turn. The true craftsman is not necessarily he who can most skilfully force his medium to obey him: equally important is his willingness to allow his medium to dictate terms to him.

ERIC NEWTON

European Painting and Sculpture

Vocabulary

potential (l. 4): which is capable of development.
circumscribed (l. 7): limited.
the law of gravity (l. 8): the force which attracts all bodies towards the centre of the earth.
inherent (l. 10): essential; those which belong to.
to dictate terms (l. 19): to tell him what he must do.

QUESTIONS

1. How does the writer amplify the statement that 'an artist's vision has no other limit than the imaginative equipment of the artist himself'? (ll. 1–2).

2. The writer makes a statement which he proves by referring to a dancer. What is the statement made?

3. Why cannot the artist have full control over his medium?

4. State in your own words what the writer means by the term 'true craftsman' (l. 16).

5. Write the general and detailed meaning of the passage and what you consider to be the writer's intention.

How it is Done

APPRECIATING ARGUMENTATIVE PROSE

In good narrative and descriptive prose, the writer may not *consciously* use what we call *devices* so as to make a carefully calculated impression on his reader. In fact, he may not be concerned with his readers' reactions at all: his sole aim may be simply to express in his own terms what he has seen or visualized. That is why this sort of writing is sometimes called 'creative'. The writer of argument, however, is in quite a different position. He can never write only to please himself. No one would write a book on, say, world affairs without having a definite audience in mind. In writing of this sort, there is no story to tell and no atmosphere to create. The aim is always to convey an idea or a number of ideas in the most effective way possible. Thus the orderly presentation of material is very important and devices are used consciously to keep the reader alert and attentive and to make difficult ideas easy to grasp. For instance contrast or illustration may be employed to jar us into thinking, or to enable us to comprehend more readily the writer's main idea.

We encounter argumentative writing almost every day of our lives in books, magazines and newspapers. More than any other type of prose, it is this sort of writing which formulates public taste and which helps people clarify their ideas about important subjects. At its best, it is stimulating and exciting prose to read—though, of course, it requires far more effort than narrative or description. At its worst, argumentative writing may deliberately mislead us or influence us in undesirable ways.

It does not follow that because devices are used consciously by writers of argument they will be immediately obvious to the reader. In good argumentative prose, devices are often far from obvious. By and large, however, it may be said that the more a writer is bent on persuading us, the more he will use devices to achieve his purpose. (In the worst forms of argument—like propaganda—the devices used are all too obvious to the discerning reader. But this sort of 'argument' does not concern us here.)

Many of the devices that are explained below will already be familiar to you, but you must always bear in mind that they are used here for quite different ends in that their purpose is to help the writer communicate his ideas. All examples illustrating their use have been drawn from passages you have studied.

STRUCTURAL DEVICES

Unity and Balance, Contrast, Illustration.

Unity and Balance. Since any argument involves careful reasoning on the part of the writer, each sentence is logically deduced from what has gone before and adds something new to the main idea. In this way the argument is gradually built until it reaches its conclusion. The usual pattern is as follows:

Statement: the main idea.

Development: proving the statement by reference to facts, or by logical deduction from what has preceded.

Conclusion: the main idea is often re-stated here, but since it has been 'proved', it obviously differs in meaning and implication from the initial statement.

The above pattern (which may be varied) gives argumentative prose its essential unity and balance. In a poorly balanced piece, the development might be out of all proportion to the statement, or conclusions might be drawn too quickly, before sufficient information has been given. The unity of a passage might be spoiled by disconnected sentences and statements which have nothing to do with the main argument.

When examining the structure of an argument, therefore, you should observe the following:

1. How far the argument follows the scheme given above or how it varies this scheme. Here you should notice whether the writer proves his argument by reference to facts or by logical deduction from his own statements.

2. Whether the argument is well balanced.

3. How the sentences are connected to one another and how each sentence adds something new to the main idea.

Your examination of the unity and balance of a piece should be written in continuous prose and in a single paragraph. The analysis you have made of a passage in order to give an account of its general and detailed meaning will help you to understand how it has been built. But you must take care *not* to repeat your detailed meaning when you are considering the structure of an argument.

Notice the balance and unity of the passage from *The Future of the Writer*. Everything that follows the initial statement ('The status of the writer is not what it was') serves to prove it. The writer blames society for this, and not the author. He begins by referring briefly to the other side of the case (that the author is to blame) but concludes that this argument 'misses the point'. The rest of the passage is devoted to showing how society has brought about this state of affairs. To do this the writer refers continually to fact (the nature of entertainment in our times and in past ages) until the ultimate conclusion is reached.

The passage from *Thinking to Some Purpose* falls into two distinct and balanced parts. The first part ('The art of persuading . . . authority') indicates what a speaker must do to persuade an audience. The second part ('If a speaker . . . ignorance') is an analysis of the danger involved. The two sections in this passage, though different in nature, are skilfully linked together by the sentence 'In the fulfilment of these needs . . . for the audience.' Furthermore, each statement in the passage is logically deduced from what has gone before. (Notice, in particular, the words the writer uses to connect the sentences: 'accordingly', 'finally', 'in the fulfilment', 'if . . . then' and 'this'.) The final statement is convincing because it has been effectively proved.

In the same way, the passage by Frieda Fordham, falls into two sections. From 'Just as it is . . . teachers' deals with parents and teachers. The latter part deals only with teachers. Each sentence develops the main idea that 'educators' must 'deepen their understanding of themselves' if they are to 'help children to develop into satisfactory men and women', and the passage is a unified and balanced whole.

Turn back to the paragraphs from *Memory* and *European Painting and Sculpture* and comment on their structure.

Contrast is often employed in argumentative prose to give more force to the main idea under discussion. A reader may grasp a point more clearly if he has been given its opposite.

In *The Future of the Writer*, J. B. Priestley contrasts the present with the past to show how society has changed. In *Thinking to Some Purpose* the contrast drawn is between the speaker and his audience; in *Psychology and Education*, it is between the teacher and the educator; in *Memory*, it is between memory and remembering; in *European Painting and Sculpture*, it is between the craftsman and his materials.

This does not mean that contrast is employed in every argument, but it does indicate how frequently writers make use of it. The reason for this is that when two opposites are placed side by side the one illumines the other. In *Thinking to Some Purpose*, for instance, it would have been impossible to outline the duties of a speaker without making any reference at all to his audience. The duties of a speaker are made all the more clear precisely because the speaker is contrasted with his audience. The same sort of thing occurs in *Memory*. Having made the 'alarming' statement that there is 'no such thing as memory', the writer goes on to draw the distinction between 'memory' and 'remembering' and to show us how easily we may confuse one with the other.

Comment briefly on the effectiveness of the contrasts drawn in the remaining passages you have studied.

Illustration. Abstract ideas are always hard to follow because it is difficult to relate them to actual experiences, things we can see and feel. For this reason writers frequently give examples drawn from everyday life to make their ideas more concrete so that they will be readily understood by the reader. Illustration often takes the form of an anecdote, a description, or a reference to some fact, and is used to emphasize a statement that would otherwise be difficult to understand. A good illustration is never given for its own sake, but so that the reader will relate it to the main argument. What a writer does, in effect, when he uses an illustration is to re-state his abstract idea in concrete, definite terms in such a way as to arouse the interest of the reader.

A good example of this occurs in *European Painting and Sculpture*. Here the writer's idea is that an artist's medium is, of its nature, limited in scope. This difficult statement immediately becomes clear when the writer gives us the example of a dancer who is 'bound by the law of gravity' and 'the nature of human anatomy'. Further on, the writer refers to the sculptor who is similarly 'bound' by his materials.

The illustration employed in *European Painting and Sculpture* is different in nature from those used in the other passages, where the examples are hypothetical (that is, they are suppositions beginning with 'If . . .') rather than actual. In *The Future of the Writer*, Priestley imagines a novelist of 'greater genius' than Dickens writing today and considers what the outcome would be. This example greatly enforces his main argument that the author is not to blame for his change of status but that times have changed and conditions are different. The writer of *Memory* similarly imagines testing an acquaintance who 'boasts of having an excellent memory'. The illustration immediately makes clear the statement that there is 'no such thing as memory'. In precisely the same way L. Susan Stebbing in *Thinking to Some Purpose* considers the effect an imaginary speaker would have on an audience if he made no effort to persuade them.

SENSE DEVICES

Style, Use of Words, Metaphor, Simile.

Style. You may have noticed when writing essays on topics which require you to argue, how difficult it is sometimes to express yourself clearly. The reason for this is that you may not have fully understood exactly what you want to say. Conversely, you will have observed how much easier it is to express yourself when you are dealing with ideas you are familiar with, or which you have thought out carefully beforehand. It may seem to you, however, that difficult subjects must be written about in a difficult way. Actually the opposite is true. When expressing complicated ideas, a writer's aim must always be to express himself as simply and as directly as possible. The quality of argumentative prose often depends on the writer's ability to convey an involved idea in a simple way so that the reader will have as little difficulty as possible in keeping up with the argument. This is why writers frequently use devices like contrast and illustration: it is part of their effort to keep the meaning simple, give variety to their expression, and so sustain the reader's interest.

When examining an argument from the point of view of style, you should observe whether the writing has been kept simple in relation to the complexity of its subject-matter. In this sense, all the passages you have studied have been written simply. The passages from *Memory* and *The Future of the Writer* may appear simpler than the others, but that is only because the argument in each case moves at a somewhat slower pace. Both writers are dealing with single subjects: memory and an author's status, and they introduce only a limited number of subsidiary ideas. The passages from *Thinking to Some Purpose* and *European Painting and Sculpture* are, on the other hand, more closely argued and thus appear more difficult. The former sets out to define the duties of a speaker and then to see what effect a speaker may have on his audience. The argument is very packed indeed and requires close reading. At the same time each idea is expressed in the simplest possible terms. In the latter, the writer brings out the limitations of different media for different arts, and considers the relation of the artist's vision to the materials at his disposal. The style is somewhat involved but never to such an extent that it obscures the writer's meaning.

Use of Words, Metaphor, Simile. Although a writer may sometimes present a whole argument in the form of a metaphor or use simile to express an idea, these two devices are not frequently to be found in argumentative prose and belong more to poetry, narrative and description. However, since they do sometimes occur, it is well to look out for them. You should also notice when a writer uses striking expressions to convey his meaning or to influence his readers.

Observe how J. B. Priestley in *The Future of the Writer* refers to authors as 'scribbling midgets'. The phrase immediately arrests our attention and, oddly enough, helps the writer to persuade us that authors are not scribbling midgets—which is what he intends. Priestley uses another means of persuasion at the end of the passage with great effect: the *rhetorical question*: that is, a question which requires no answer: 'We have our post-war public figures, but how many of them are authors?' The question is made effective because of the argument that has preceded it.

In the passage from *Memory*, the words chosen are deliberately kept simple so that the reader will understand that memory does not exist. This is fully conveyed when memory is compared to a 'big toe'. Frieda Fordham, in *Psychology and Education*, does something similar when she uses the colloquial phrase 'stuff them with knowledge' to bring out the differences between her conception of a 'teacher' and an 'educator'.

The way language is handled will always vary with the argument. Do not be surprised if in some argumentative passages you find that there is little to say about the writer's use of words, as there is less need in this type of prose to strive after striking verbal effects.

EXERCISES ON APPRECIATION

[1]

The objection to most amateur science lies not in the foolishness of its experiments, but in the inability of the experimenters to be satisfied with negative results. Most laboratory experiments are failures, and even when an apparent success has been obtained the competent researcher at once tries to catch himself out. I am going to waste tomorrow on an experiment which I hope and trust will be a failure, for if it were a success it would not

only be quite inexplicable, but would destroy the
theoretical results of a year's work. Amateur scientists 10
commonly fail because they set out to prove something
rather than to arrive at the truth, whatever it may be.
They do not realize that a good half of most research
work consists in an attempt to prove yourself wrong.
Intellectual honesty is discouraged by politics, religion, 15
and even courtesy. It is the hardest but the most essential
of the habits which the scientist, whether professional or
amateur, must form. And if he can spread the habit
among his fellow men it may prove to be a contribution
to the good life compared to which the applications of 20
science to engineering and medicine are comparatively
unimportant.

J. B. S. HALDANE

Possible Worlds

Vocabulary

apparent (l. 5): seeming.
competent researcher (ll. 5–6): skilled person who is trying
to discover new facts.
tries to catch himself out (l. 6): tries to catch himself making a
mistake.

QUESTIONS

1. Give the general and detailed meaning of the passage and
what you consider to be the writer's intention.

2. In what way are the writer's conclusions related to his initial
statement?

3. Comment on the way the sentences are connected to one
another.

4. What use is made of illustration in this passage?

5. Is the writer's style involved or simple? Give reasons for your
answer.

[2]

Sometimes justification may be sought for the deliberate imposition of mental or physical pain on the criminal in the argument that it is right the wicked should suffer for their transgressions as a form of expiation. If this is a genuine conviction, and not merely the desire for 5 revenge masquerading under a more reputable cloak, it seems to regard 'crime' and 'sin' as synonymous terms. It is true that most major crimes are also sins, but it is not because of their sinfulness that the State punishes them, but because they are inimical to the stability and 10 welfare of the community. If it is a moral law that sin should be expiated by suffering, it still does not necessarily follow that it is the function of the State to ensure this. It is a matter rather for forces other than those emanating from man-made law. The State has no yard- 15 stick to measure degrees of sin; such measurement would demand an insight into the working of the human soul that no judge or magistrate on the Bench would dare to claim.

WINIFRED A. ELKIN

The English Penal System

Vocabulary

transgressions (l. 4): breaking the law.

a form of expiation (l. 4): a way of making up for the wrong they have done.

conviction (l. 5): belief.

masquerading (l. 6): disguising itself.

inimical (l. 10): hostile to, acting against.

emanating (l. 15): having their source in, issuing from.

yardstick (ll. 15–16): standard.

insight (l. 17): understanding.

on the Bench (l. 18): on the judge's seat. In this sense 'in the act of judging'.

QUESTIONS

1. Give the general and detailed meaning of the passage and what you consider to be the writer's intention.

2. Comment on the structure of the passage.

3. Explain how the writer draws a contrast between 'crime' and 'sin'.

4. Which statement in the passage indicates that man-made law is not the same as moral law?

5. Comment on the writer's style.

[3]

The history of science could never be adequately reconstructed by a student who confined his attention to the few men of supreme genius. We should produce a misleading diagram of the whole course of things if we merely drew direct lines from one of these mighty peaks 5 to another. The great books are undoubtedly preferable to the reader, more serviceable in education and more enriching to the mind; but, if we restrict ourselves to these, the result is likely to be a rope of sand; and in any case this is not the way in which to make discoveries in 10 the history of any science. In reality, the technical historian, bent on discovery—proceeding therefore from the known to the unknown—tends to find himself drawn rather in the opposite direction. Aware of the importance of Sir Isaac Newton, he strains to see what 15 was the state of science in the period before Newton took hold of his problems. He follows the history of gravitation—not excluding the mistakes and misfires— down to the moment when the famous apple fell. And, in reality, only in this way can anybody take the measure 20 of what Newton himself achieved.

HERBERT BUTTERFIELD

Man on His Past

Vocabulary

> a misleading diagram (ll. 3–4): a picture which gives us the wrong impression.
>
> strains (l. 15): makes every possible effort to.
>
> gravitation (l. 18): gravity, the force by which bodies are attracted towards the earth's centre or towards one another.

QUESTIONS

1. Give the general and detailed meaning of the passage and what you consider to be the writer's intention.
2. Show how the writer achieves balance in this passage.
3. What illustration is used and what is its purpose?
4. Show how the writer achieves connection between his sentences.
5. Explain the function of these three metaphors: 'if we merely drew direct lines from one of these mighty peaks to another' (ll 4–6); 'rope of sand' (l. 9); 'misfires' (l. 18).

Literary Appreciation

Your appreciation of the passages that follow must be written in continuous prose and clearly divided into paragraphs. When noting how a piece has been written, never make comments without referring to the text; if necessary, quote the writer's own words. You should, furthermore, make every effort to show how the structure of a piece and the sense devices employed serve to convey the main point of the argument.

A brief recapitulation of the method you have learned follows below:

KEY

1. READING	Read the passage several times until you are sure of its meaning.
2. MEANING	*General*: often the opening sentence.
	Detailed: the main stages of the argument.
	Intention

3. DEVICES

(a) STRUCTURAL	*Unity and Balance*: (Statement, Development, Conclusion.)	
	Contrast	
	Illustration	
(b) SENSE	*Style*	
	Use of Words, metaphor, simile	

Study this appreciation of the passage from *Thinking to Some Purpose* before going on to write appreciations of your own. Your work should be along these lines.

The writer analyses the way a speaker should persuade an audience into believing something and points out some of the dangers involved in the fulfilment of this purpose.

What the writer first considers is *how* a speaker should address an audience. A speaker, she says, should keep his hearers interested, repeat himself to make his points clear, avoid expressing himself in a monotonous way, and speak with an air of authority. The necessity for such tactics gives rise to dangers for both the speaker and his audience. The danger for a speaker is that he will fail to persuade his hearers if he ignores these precepts and makes no appeal to emotion. On the other hand, a speaker may abuse the means of persuasion at his disposal and thus get his audience to believe anything he says.

The writer's intention is to make us think about the problems involved in public speaking and the dangers that face both a speaker and his audience.

In developing her argument, the writer considers her main idea from two angles. Down to the word 'authority' (l. 14) the initial statement, that a speaker should use various tactics to persuade his audience, is amplified. Then the writer goes on to examine what would happen if a speaker ignored the tactics outlined or made too great a use of them. Even though the argument falls into two distinct parts, it is very well balanced and controlled. The sentence 'In the fulfilment of these needs . . . audience' immediately links

F

what has preceded with what follows, so that there is no sharp break in thought. Every sentence is, moreover, logically deduced from the one that goes before. Words and phrases like 'accordingly', 'finally', 'in the fulfilment', 'if . . . then', and 'this' all indicate the writer's methods of deducing one idea from another and building up an argument. The whole passage is thus closely argued and completely unified with the result that we are given a very clear account indeed of the problem under discussion.

Throughout the passage, the writer contrasts the speaker with the audience. A good example of this occurs in the illustration the writer gives where she imagines a speaker failing to employ any tactics at all and considers the effect this would have on the hearers. In this way, the point that there are 'great temptations for the speaker and grave dangers for the audience' is fully brought out.

Though the problem dealt with is a very complicated one, the writer's style is straightforward so that difficult ideas are reduced to simple terms. This clear and orderly presentation of ideas enables the reader to understand the nature of the problem discussed and encourages him to think about it.

Write an appreciation of each of the passages that follow.

[1]

When we think of the sufferings of human beings and animals at the hands—if that is the right word—of insects, we feel that it is pardonable enough to make faces at creatures so inconsiderate. But what strikes one as remarkable is that the insects that do man most harm   5
are not those that horrify him most. A lady who will sit bravely while a wasp hangs in the air and inspects first her right and then her left temple will run a mile from a harmless spider. Another will remain collected (though murderous) in presence of a horsefly, but will shudder at   10
the sight of a moth that is innocent of blood. Our fears, it is evident, do not march in all respects with our sense of physical danger. There are insects that make us feel

that we are in the presence of the uncanny. Many of us
have this feeling about moths. Moths are the ghosts of 15
the insect world. It may be the manner in which they
flutter in unheralded out of the night that terrifies us.
They seem to tap against our lighted windows as though
the outer darkness had a message for us. And their
persistence helps to terrify. They are more troublesome 20
than a subject nation. They are more importunate than
the importunate widow. But they are most terrifying of
all if one suddenly sees their eyes blazing crimson as they
catch the light. One thinks of nocturnal rites in an
African forest temple and of terrible jewels blazing in 25
the head of an evil goddess—jewels to be stolen, we
realize, by a foolish white man, thereafter to be the
object of a vendetta in a sensational novel. One feels
that one's hair would be justified in standing on end,
only that hair does not do such things. The sight of a 30
moth's eye is, I fancy, a rare one for most people. It is
a sight one can no more forget than a house on fire.

ROBERT LYND

Why we hate Insects

Vocabulary

    uncanny (l. 14): mysterious, supernatural.
    unheralded (l. 17): their approach not having been announced.
    importunate (l. 21): persistent, demanding.
    vendetta (l. 28): blood-feud in which the injured party seek
      vengeance on the offender.

[2]

The Englishman appears to be cold and unemotional
because he is really slow. When an event happens, he
may understand it quickly enough with his mind, but he
takes quite a while to feel it. Once upon a time a coach,
containing some Englishmen and some Frenchmen, was 5
driving over the Alps. The horses ran away, and as they
were dashing across a bridge the coach caught on the

stonework, tottered, and nearly fell into the ravine below. The Frenchmen were frantic with terror: they
screamed and gesticulated and flung themselves about, 10
as Frenchmen would. The Englishmen sat quite calm.
An hour later the coach drew up at an inn to change
horses, and by that time the situations were exactly
reversed. The Frenchmen had forgotten all about the
danger, and were chattering gaily; the Englishmen had 15
just begun to feel it, and one had a nervous breakdown
and was obliged to go to bed. We have here a clear
physical difference between the two races—a difference
that goes deep into character. The Frenchmen responded
at once; the Englishmen responded in time. They were 20
slow and they were also practical. Their instinct forbade
them to throw themselves about in the coach, because
it was more likely to tip over if they did. They had this
extraordinary appreciation of *fact* that we shall notice
again and again. When a disaster comes, the English 25
instinct is to do what can be done first, and to postpone
the feeling as long as possible. Hence they are splendid
at emergencies. No doubt they are brave—no one will
deny that—but bravery is partly an affair of the nerves,
and the English nervous system is well equipped for 30
meeting a physical emergency. It acts promptly and feels
slowly. Such a combination is fruitful, and anyone who
possesses it has gone a long way toward being brave.
And when the action is over, then the Englishman can
feel.   35

E. M. FORSTER

Abinger Harvest

Vocabulary

tottered (l. 8): swayed from side to side as if it was going to
fall.
gesticulated (l. 10): waved their arms.

[3]

Every man who has acquired some unusual skill enjoys exercising it until it has become a matter of course,
or until he can no longer improve himself. This motive
to activity begins in early childhood: a boy who can
stand on his head becomes reluctant to stand on his feet.   5
A great deal of work gives the same pleasure that is to be
derived from games of skill. The work of a lawyer or a
politician must contain in a more delectable form a great
deal of the same pleasure that is to be derived from playing bridge. Here of course there is not only the exercise   10
of skill but the outwitting of a skilled opponent. Even
where this competitive element is absent, however, the
performance of difficult feats is agreeable. A man who
can do stunts in an aeroplane finds the pleasure so great
that for the sake of it he is willing to risk his life. I   15
imagine that an able surgeon, in spite of the painful
circumstances in which his work is done, derives satis-
faction from the exquisite precision of his operations.
The same kind of pleasure, though in a less intense
form, is to be derived from a great deal of work of a   20
humbler kind. All skilled work can be pleasurable, provided the skill required is either variable or capable of
indefinite improvement. If these conditions are absent,
it will cease to be interesting when a man has acquired
his maximum skill. A man who runs three-mile races   25
will cease to find pleasure in this occupation when he
passes the age at which he can beat his own previous
record. Fortunately there is a very considerable amount
of work in which new circumstances call for new skill
and a man can go on improving, at any rate until he has   30
reached middle age. In some kinds of skilled work, such
as politics, for example, it seems that men are at their
best between sixty and seventy, the reason being that in
such occupations a wide experience of other men is
essential. For this reason successful politicians are apt to 35
be happier at the age of seventy than any other men of

equal age. Their only competitors in this respect are the men who are the heads of big businesses.

BERTRAND RUSSELL

The Conquest of Happiness

Vocabulary

a matter of course (l. 2): something which he does quite naturally.

delectable (l. 8): delightful.

outwitting (l. 11): getting the better of, defeating.

stunts (l. 14): spectacular tricks done for effect.

apt (l. 35): inclined.

[4]

Though it may be unessential to the imagination, travel is necessary to an understanding of men. Only with long experience and the opening of his wares on many a beach where his language is not spoken, will the merchant come to know the worth of what he 5 carries, and what is parochial and what is universal in his choice. Such delicate goods as justice, love and honour, courtesy, and indeed all the things we care for, are valid everywhere; but they are variously moulded and often differently handled, and sometimes nearly 10 unrecognizable if you meet them in a foreign land; and the art of learning fundamental common values is perhaps the greatest gain of travel to those who wish to live at ease among their fellows.

Beyond this and above all is enjoyment with no 15 utilitarian objective, which it is the main business of both travel and education to increase as they can. Good days are to be gathered like sunshine in grapes, to be trodden and bottled into wine and kept for age to sip at ease beside his fire. If the traveller has vintaged well 20 he need trouble to wander no longer; the ruby moments glow in his glass at will. He can still feel the spring in his step, and the wind on his face, though he sit in shelter: unless perhaps the sight of a long road winding,

or the singing of the telegraph wires, or the wild duck in 25
their wedges, or horses' hooves that clatter into distance,
or the wayside stream—all with their many voices persuade him to try just one more journey before the pleasant world comes to an end.

FREYA STARK

Perseus in the Wind

Vocabulary

> unessential (l. 1): 'inessential' is the more usual form.
> parochial (l. 6): of purely local interest.
> moulded (l. 9): formed.
> no utilitarian objective (ll. 15-16): which does not aim at being
> useful.
> trodden (l. 19): past participle of 'tread', crushed under the
> feet.
> vintaged (l. 20): 'matured'.

[5]

There have been so many misunderstandings about
modern architecture that before we begin to discuss
what it is, it may be as well to mention a few things that
it is not. It is not, for one thing, a fashionable style of
jazz ornament; it is not the custom of building in con- 5
crete, or with flat roofs and horizontal window-panes;
it is not 'functionalism'. It *is* quite simply, like all good
architecture, the honest product of science and art. It
aims at once more relating methods of building as
closely as possible to real needs. In fact it is nothing 10
more or less than the exact modern equivalent of the
architecture that flourished in previous ages, but fell
into decay during the last century through architects
having got out of touch with life and having forgotten
what architecture was really for. 15

There are several other reasons why it is important
just now for the man in the street to understand a little
more what modern architecture is all about, besides the
reason of satisfying his own curiosity and justifying the

architects who produce it. One reason is that, like all   20
movements that contain something new as well as something important, the modern movement in architecture
acquired a following of imitators: vulgarizers who joined
up with the movement only in order to cash in, as it
were, on its news value. To this category belong all the   25
makers of jazz-modern shop fronts in chromium plate
and glass, all the purveyors of smart angular furniture
and all the builders of nasty 'modernistic' villas; people
who have no understanding of modern architecture's
ideals, but who could not have come into being without   30
it. This bogus modernism, whether it is the result of
the commercial exploitation of novelty or merely the
wish to be in the fashion, has done great harm to the
cause of good modern architecture by bringing it into
disrepute. And the only way to prevent the fine ideals of   35
the one from being vulgarized into insignificance by the
other is for people to discriminate better between them.
If people understand the point of genuine modern architecture and appreciate what it is trying to do, they will
see quickly enough that the ungenuine—which is often   40
called 'modernistic'—has no basis beyond itself. It consists only of a few flashy tricks and the use (often the
wrong use) of a number of fashionable materials.

J. M. RICHARDS

An Introduction to
Modern Architecture

Vocabulary

'functionalism' (l. 7): i.e., constructing buildings which are
useful rather than beautiful.

to cash in . . . on (ll. 24–5): to make money out of.

purveyors (l. 27): sellers.

bogus (l. 31): sham, false.

bringing it into disrepute (ll. 34–5): giving it a bad name.

vulgarized into insignificance (l. 36): being made so vulgar
that they no longer have any value.

flashy (l. 42): smart on the surface but really worthless.

[6]

Society never advances. It recedes as fast on one side as it gains on the other. It undergoes continual changes; it is barbarous, it is civilized, it is christianized, it is rich, it is scientific; but this change is not amelioration. For everything that is given something is taken. Society 5 acquires new arts and loses old instincts. What a contrast between the well-clad, reading, writing, thinking American, with a watch, a pencil and a bill of exchange in his pocket, and the naked New Zealander, whose property is a club, a spear, a mat and an undivided twentieth of a 10 shed to sleep under! But compare the health of the two men and you shall see that the white man has lost his aboriginal strength. If the traveller tell us truly, strike the savage with a broadaxe and in a day or two the flesh shall unite and heal as if you struck the blow into soft 15 pitch, and the same blow shall send the white to his grave.

The civilized man has built a coach, but has lost the use of his feet. He is supported on crutches, but lacks so much support of muscle. He has a fine Geneva watch, 20 but he fails of the skill to tell the hour by the sun. A Greenwich nautical almanac he has, and so being sure of the information when he wants it, the man in the street does not know a star in the sky. The solstice he does not observe; the equinox he knows as little; and 25 the whole bright calendar of the year is without a dial in his mind. His notebooks impair his memory; his libraries overload his wit; the insurance office increases the number of accidents; and it may be a question whether machinery does not encumber; whether we 30 have not lost by refinement some energy, by a Christianity, entrenched in establishments and forms, some vigour of wild virtue.

RALPH WALDO EMERSON

Self-Reliance

Vocabulary

amelioration (l. 4): improvement.

well-clad (l. 7): well-dressed.

aboriginal (l. 13): primitive.

crutches (l. 19): wooden supports used by people who are lame.

almanac (l. 22): annual calendar of months and days.

solstice (l. 24): time at which the sun is farthest from the equator.

equinox (l. 25): time at which the sun crosses the equator.

without a dial in his mind (ll. 26–7): i.e., he cannot picture it in his mind.

impair (l. 27): weaken.

encumber (l. 30): weigh us down.

entrenched (l. 32): surrounded by and protected from attack.

[7]

It may be said that all understanding of the universe comes from the combined action of two faculties in us, the power to register impressions and the capacity to reason and reflect on them. Understanding would be increased if we could succeed in increasing the efficiency 5 of either of these components of knowledge. It is highly suggestive that the only method of increasing understanding which is ever made use of in the West is that of heightening our capacity to register impressions. This is done by using instruments such as the telescope and the 10 microscope which extend our vision a thousandfold and bring to the eye undulations of light which without their aid would never reach the retina. No attempt is ever made in the West to improve the working of that part of our psychic equipment which reasons and reflects, for 15 it is generally believed that this cannot be altered. It is recognized of course that different men vary in the ability to make associations, to draw distinctions and to reason, but no effort is ever made to increase the capacity of the individual man to reason and reflect. Western 20

systems of psychology and philosophy show but little
interest in the particular quality of mind which distinguishes a man from animals, the quality of consciousness. Because of this failure to study this special attribute
of man, it is assumed that the reflecting and reasoning   25
capacity of the human mind is unalterable. All therefore
that we are believed to be capable of doing, if we want to
learn more of the world in which we live, is to multiply
the messages we receive from it in the belief that if we
can see more we shall also be able to understand more.   30
But unfortunately the mere enlargement of the windows
through which messages reach us from without does not
necessarily lead to an increase of understanding and as
often as not it results only in an increase of confusion.

KENNETH WALKER

Meaning and Purpose

Vocabulary

components (l. 6): essential parts.
undulations (l. 12): waves.
retina (l. 13): part of the eye that is sensitive to light.
psychic (l. 15): which has to do with the spirit.
attribute (l. 24): quality.

[8]

When we admire aesthetically the marvellous masonry
and architecture of the Great Pyramid or the exquisite
furniture and jewellery of Tut-ankh-Amen's tomb, there
is a conflict in our hearts between our pride and pleasure
in such triumphs of human art and our moral condemna-   5
tion of the human price at which these triumphs have
been bought: the hard labour unjustly imposed on the
many to produce the fine flowers of civilization for the
exclusive enjoyment of a few who reap where they have
not sown. During these last five or six thousand years,   10
the masters of the civilizations have robbed their slaves
of their share in the fruits of society's corporate labours
as cold-bloodedly as we rob our bees of their honey. The

moral ugliness of the unjust act mars the aesthetic beauty of the artistic result; yet, up till now, the few 15 favoured beneficiaries of civilization have had one obvious common-sense plea to put forward in their own defence. It has been a choice, they have been able to plead, between fruits of civilization for the few and no fruits at all. Our technological command over nature is 20 severely limited. We have at our command neither sufficient muscle-power nor sufficient labour to turn out our amenities in more than minute quantities. If I am to deny these to myself just because you cannot all have them too, we shall have to shut up shop and allow one 25 of the finest talents of human nature to rust away buried in a napkin; and, while that is certainly not in my interest, it is surely not in yours either on a longer view. For I am not enjoying this monopoly of amenities exclusively for my own benefit. My enjoyment is at least 30 partly vicarious. In indulging myself at your expense, I am in some sense serving as a kind of trustee for all future generations of the whole human race. This plea was a plausible one, even in our technologically go-ahead Western world, down to the eighteenth century inclu- 35 sive, but our unprecedented technological progress in the last hundred and fifty years has made the same plea invalid today.

ARNOLD J. TOYNBEE
Civilization on Trial

Vocabulary

aesthetically (l. 1): by appreciating its beauty.
masonry (l. 1): stonework.
exclusive (l. 9): sole.
corporate (l. 12): combined.
mars (l. 14): spoils.
beneficiaries (l. 16): those who have benefited.
amenities (l. 23): things that give us pleasure; benefits.
vicarious (l. 31): for the benefit of others.
indulging (l. 31): enjoying.

trustee (l. 32): in this sense, one who has the responsibility of preserving the amenities.

the plea was a plausible one (ll. 33–4): the excuse seemed on the surface to be a reasonable one.

unprecedented (l. 36): which has never been known before.